Praise for
I'm Pregnant . . .
Now What?

This book is exceptional! It is a real godsend for churches and the clergy, and I will be sharing it with my fellow clergy.

BISHOP DAVID ABE
Jerusalem Catholic Church
Richmond, Virginia

An incredibly insightful collection of stories and shared bits of wisdom to help any young woman who finds herself unexpectedly pregnant. A book that looks at unplanned pregnancies honestly and helps you find your way through the maze of confusion.

DELILAH
Adoptive mother and hostess of syndicated radio show, Delilah

With insight, encouragement and practical guidelines, Ruth Graham and Dr. Sara Dormon go step-by-step through the many layers of decisions that have to be made in the event of an unplanned pregnancy. This is a resource much needed in our culture.

RYAN DOBSON
Speaker/Author

In this book, you will find encouragement, practical help and, most of all, hope. Sara Dormon and my daughter, Ruth, speak honestly out of their own experiences.

RUTH BELL GRAHAM
Author and wife of evangelist Billy Graham

God says in His Word that no one is a mistake. *I'm Pregnant, Now What?* explores all sides of a profoundly difficult subject with compassionate insight, honest disclosure, solid biblical advice and realistic life-affirming options. In my opinion, experience overrides theory, and I applaud Ruth, Windsor and Sara for their willingness to candidly help others by way of their personal journeys. Bravo!

JENNIFER O'NEILL
Model and Actress

I'm Pregnant . . . Now What?

RUTH GRAHAM
&
SARA R. DORMON, PH.D.

Regal

From Gospel Light
Ventura, California, U.S.A.

PUBLISHED BY REGAL BOOKS
FROM GOSPEL LIGHT
VENTURA, CALIFORNIA, U.S.A.
PRINTED IN THE U.S.A.

Regal Books is a ministry of Gospel Light, a Christian publisher dedicated to serving the local church. We believe God's vision for Gospel Light is to provide church leaders with biblical, user-friendly materials that will help them evangelize, disciple and minister to children, youth and families.

It is our prayer that this Regal book will help you discover biblical truth for your own life and help you meet the needs of others. May God richly bless you.

For a free catalog of resources from Regal Books/Gospel Light, please call your Christian supplier or contact us at 1-800-4-GOSPEL or www.regalbooks.com.

Previously published by ForPregnancyHelp.com in 2002.

All Scripture quotations, unless otherwise indicated, are taken from the *Holy Bible, New International Version*®. Copyright © 1973, 1978, 1984 by International Bible Society. Used by permission of Zondervan Publishing House. All rights reserved.

Other version used is
KJV—King James Version. Authorized King James Version.

To protect the privacy of some of the individuals whose stories are shared in this book, names have been changed. With permission, real names and events are portrayed in most of the stories.

ForPregnancyHelp.com edition published in 2002.
Regal Books edition published in October 2004.

Cover design by David Griffing
Edited by Kathy Deering

Library of Congress Cataloging-in-Publication Data
Graham, Ruth, 1950–
    I'm pregnant . . . now what? / Ruth Graham and Sara Dormon.
      p. cm.
    ISBN 0-8307-3575-5
    1. Pregnant women—Religious life. 2. Pregnancy—Religious aspects—Christianity.
I. Dormon, Sara. II. Title.
BV4529.18.G73 2004
248.8'431—dc22   2004015888

1   2   3   4   5   6   7   8   9   10   /   10   09   08   07   06   05   04

Rights for publishing this book in other languages are contracted by Gospel Light Worldwide, the international nonprofit ministry of Gospel Light. Gospel Light Worldwide also provides publishing and technical assistance to international publishers dedicated to producing Sunday School and Vacation Bible School curricula and books in the languages of the world. For additional information, visit www.gospellightworldwide.org; write to Gospel Light Worldwide, P.O. Box 3875, Ventura, CA 93006; or send an e-mail to info@gospellightworldwide.org.

Dedication

To life and all those who choose it.

Contents

Acknowledgments

Someone once said, "When you see a turtle on a fence post, you know he didn't get there by himself." The same can be said of this book. We have many people to thank for their contributions to the book and their support of us.

The list of people who encouraged, guided, taught, loved and supported us begins with our families. They put up with missed meals, absent mothers and grouchy wives, all the while expressing their pride at what we were doing. Bill, Peter, David, Windsor and Wyatt, you are all the best and we love you. To our circle of friends who have listened, laughed, cried with us and fed us as we wrote, we love you, thank you and honor you.

To Cherie, Joy and Mary, your courage, honesty and love for your children are testimony to us all. You are among the bravest and most courageous of women. Without you and those who share your journey, this book would not have been written.

Windsor, you inspire us, amaze us and make us proud to be part of your life. Thank you for your willingness to share your story so that others may benefit from it.

To Jennifer O'Neill and Hunter Tylo, two women of amazing grace and conviction, your honesty and vulnerability lights the path for many who have been wounded by abortion. Keep speaking out.

Kevin and Heather, parents of Brynne, Grace and Dylan. What can we say except that your contribution brings tears to our eyes and helps us to see adoption for what it really is—a miracle orchestrated by God. Thank you for your open hearts and home and for so easily sharing your story with so many.

Brown and Giselle, parents of Joy, friends to many and counselors to more. What a journey and what an honor to have shared it with you. You are examples to all as to how parents of teens with unplanned pregnancies should behave. You modeled Christ to us all, and we will never forget you for it.

Frank Lunn, adopted child, author of *Stacking the Logs*, and a man with an amazing story, thank you for sharing your wisdom and feelings on being adopted and your words of encouragement to birthmothers and adoptive parents.

Tim Troyer, your chapter on how the Church should respond to the pregnant girl and her family is incredible. You have said what needs to be said and have set the bar exactly where it should be set for pastors and churches that encounter this situation. Thank you for your spirit and obedience to our Lord.

Kathy Deering, editor, encourager, supporter and friend, who gently but consistently walked with us down the road to completion, this book would not be what it is without your having been a part of it. "Thank you" are not big enough words for what you have meant to us and this process.

To Bill Harrison, your passion for our mission has been a constant in this entire journey and we thank you for the time, energy, vision and commitment you have had for us and to us.

And finally, the members of our "new family" at Regal Books. Kim Bangs, a woman of conviction, commitment and compassion. Thank you for your willingness to take on this project and support us in our dream by putting feet on it. Bill Greig III, president of Regal and a man on whom we can call and lean and from whom we will continue to learn. Your love of the Lord and commitment to authors radiates in your words and actions. Bill Denzel, vice president of marketing, your support for us and this book has made the process a pleasure. And to Marlene Baer, your ideas and heart for the young women we are trying to reach inspires us. Mia Kaely, Deena Davis, David Griffing and the rest of the team, thank you for your special gifts and talents you have brought to this project. To all of you, a heartfelt thank-you for helping us bring this "baby" to term.

As the two of us have helped each other overcome many challenges, including the writing of this book, our friendship, love and respect for each other have deepened greatly.

Introduction

This book comes out of experience. We have been where you are. Many people have helped us write this book, and they all understand what you are going through.

If you are reading this page, you are full of questions for which you have few, if any, answers. People may be giving you answers, but they don't really know your questions and don't seem to be listening to you. You are under too much stress and pressure. You may be alone in your dilemma with no support from people who made you promises. You feel rejected and betrayed. You are hurt and angry. We understand those feelings.

It is our desire to address your needs factually and to encourage you. We will examine from all sides the issues involved and give you the best information available so that you can make a decision with which you can live. We believe that an informed decision is the best decision and that you have the right to make your own decisions. The decisions you make will have long-term ramifications that affect not only you and your baby but others as well. We want to let you hear from other young women who were faced with an unplanned pregnancy. What were their choices and how did their decisions affect them? These are real people in real-life situations. Their stories are told objectively so that you can draw your own conclusions.

We believe that God gives us choice and that He asks us to choose life. We believe that God creates every baby and that while we were yet in our mothers' wombs He knew our bodies, our personalities, our temperaments and our minds. We believe the Scriptures teach that life is sacred, a gift from God that is to be respected as holy and valuable. Life is life even when it is the result of rape, even when the child is deformed and even when it threatens the life of the mother. It is life.

It is out of our commitment to life that we encourage young women to carry their unborn children to life—there is no greater love. We know it is a costly decision emotionally, physically and mentally.

And yet we know that the world is an imperfect place and we are confronted with difficult choices every day. God knows our frames and remembers we are but dust and extends to us forgiveness of sin, mercy for healing and grace for living. We do not condemn those who choose differently. In fact, it is our commitment to love and encourage those who have been deeply wounded by abortion.

We support the adoption option wholeheartedly, but we believe with equal passion that there must be long-term support for birthmothers. This is what this book is about—supporting and encouraging the birthmother, regardless of the choice she makes. We are not interested in politics, but in lives—the lives of young women and men who have made mistakes and who now face difficult decisions. "Greater love has no one than this, that he lay down his life for his friends" (John 15:13).

I'm Pregnant . . . Now What?

Ruth

My daughter Windsor had been sleeping a lot. She would come home from school and take a long nap before dragging herself down to dinner.

She had been keeping company with a young man who was pleasant but who had few, if any, ambitions. I had not prevented them from seeing each other, but I certainly hoped their relationship would soon run its course.

When Windsor was younger, she had enjoyed horseback riding, but she had dropped her interest when boys began to appeal to her. For a time, she had seemed to enjoy flight lessons, but then this young man had diverted her attention. I had encouraged her to get involved in sports, so she had tried out for basketball. But she did not make the team. Now she had fallen in with a crowd that had little ambition except to have a big truck and plenty of chewing tobacco. Naturally, I had higher aspirations for her. Windsor accused me of being judgmental and not trusting her. Our relationship became volatile and frustrating. I was keenly disappointed and even questioned God about these developments.

One sunny November afternoon, Windsor came and sat beside me on my bed. I saw fear in her big blue eyes as she confessed that she suspected she was pregnant.

My mind raced. I tried to prepare myself for what lay ahead as I embraced her, telling her it would be okay. I wanted to stay calm. Inwardly I was far from confident, and outwardly my mind began to shift into overdrive as more adrenaline kicked in.

I was oddly reluctant to have her suspicion confirmed and I might have let it go for several days, if not weeks. (Denial is an amazing thing!) I was not sure that I was ready to deal with all that might come if we found out for sure. But after Windsor went to school the next day, I confided in a friend and she urged us to go that very afternoon for a pregnancy test.

So after school, I drove Windsor to the doctor's office. My mind raced ahead. *How would we handle this? Could I protect her? And what about my own reputation? What would people say now?* I was a single mom, and I could hear blame being cast in my direction. What was I supposed to *do?* I really was not prepared for this. This was not supposed to happen in the Graham family.

The doctor confirmed that Windsor was pregnant. Still in his office, I looked into her eyes brimming with tears and held her tightly as moans escaped from her inner depths. My mind continued to race. *How could I help her?*

Our lives had just been changed forever.

Big Decisions

I knew Windsor was wounded already and did not need me to add salt to her wounds. I knew that she was feeling guilty and ashamed and that I should not add to it. I could see that her father's neglect and the upheaval in our home as a result of the divorce had left a hole in her heart that she was trying to fill by "looking for love in all the wrong places." She did not need more rejection from me.

As a mother, what do you do with the information that your 16-year-old daughter is pregnant? I could not hide it under a rock for long. I could not ignore it and hope it would go away. I could not shout it from the rooftops or run around in circles screaming. At some point, sooner rather than later, I would have to confront the many issues involved. Ultimately, this would involve facing my own responsibility, guilt, shame and anger. In spite of my love, tears, prayers and efforts at discipline (sometimes yelling a lot), my child had made bad choices with serious consequences. Should I have done more? Watched more closely? Grounded her more often? (Yes, no doubt I could have become her jailer—and that only would have made the situation worse.)

To ease my confusion, I reached for a devotional book and it opened to Bible verses about peace. Peace! I was so far from being peaceful. But it was exactly the word I needed. As I read "The Lord of peace himself gives you peace always by all means. The Lord be with you all" (2 Thess. 3:16, *KJV*) and "My presence shall go with thee" (Exod. 33:14, *KJV*), I felt a peace that was not my own. I would return to those verses many times.

I was the adult. My child needed my help. I could not come unglued. My tears would have to come much later. We both needed to stop and take a breath, to think and to pray and to get counsel. We did not know what to do, and I needed to find someone who could help us sort it all out.

Windsor made the first big decision herself—she did not want an abortion. I was thankful for that.

Windsor also informed her boyfriend of her pregnancy. He said he did not love her and did not want to marry her. He was as young and scared as she was. Windsor and I met with him and his mother, together with a licensed counselor. The young man met with us several more times and was honest about his feelings, although it cut Windsor to ribbons. The more he withdrew from her, the more desperate she became in trying to hold on to him. It wasn't long before he was gone.

I made hundreds of phone calls. I called the local juvenile court officer to find out the legal issues and what responsibility the young man had for this child. Since Windsor was only 16, I inquired about statutory rape, but it did not apply in her case. I asked if I could keep the young man away from Windsor. There were legal ways to do that. I learned that the young man could be entitled to visitation and would have a financial responsibility until the baby was 18 years old.

I called a local crisis pregnancy center to find out what resources they offered. Their counselors met with Windsor a few times. We found them to be very understanding and helpful. The center gave me names of unwed mothers' homes and I pursued each lead, although the homes I called were either far away or seemed to be too rigid. Windsor had heard enough preaching. What she needed now was a balanced approach, cushioned with a sense of humor. I didn't want to send her to some grim place. After all, this was life, not death. Everywhere I turned there seemed to be hidden—or not-so-hidden—agendas. Most agencies

I called believed that young women should release their babies for adoption—only a few believed that the choice belonged to the young woman. Windsor did not want to be manipulated into a decision. The search was frustrating.

I called a pastor. He prescribed the following advice: a child was coming, the young couple involved was not capable of taking care of it and strict ground rules should be set for Windsor; namely, carry to term, quit seeing the young man and deal with the sin of the situation. The options he offered included (1) Windsor and the young man could move in together, (2) they could drop out of school and get jobs in preparation for marriage and the baby, or (3) they could release the baby for adoption. If they decided to marry, he told me the marriage would likely not survive since 95 percent of couples who marry under these circumstances split up and those who remain married report they are unhappy and wish they had married someone else.

The pastor suggested a meeting with Windsor, the young man and his mother, Windsor's father and me. We met on a Sunday after church. Windsor was surprised to see her father, who had flown in from where he lived in Texas. In fact, she was angry and upset and declared she would have no part in the meeting.

After coaxing, eventually she joined us. The pastor gave the young couple his set of options: They could move in together without marriage or get jobs and marry—or Windsor could go to a home for unwed mothers. The young man told us all that he had no way of supporting her, he admitted that he did not love her and found her difficult to get along with, and finally, he declared that he did not want to marry her. Windsor was deeply hurt by the finality of his betrayal. At the same time, she was shocked and angered that the minister had suggested she move in with the young man without being married. She balked at the suggestion of going to a home for unwed mothers. She exploded. She felt trapped. The meeting was a disaster! The birthfather walked away seemingly scot-free while his former girlfriend's whole life was turned upside down. Windsor keenly felt the unfairness of it all.

For my part, I felt exhausted and beat-up after the meeting. At odds with my own emotions, I was both angry with Windsor, wanting to shake her, and compassionate, longing to hold her and make everything all right. She could not seem to see that I was trying to help. Worn out with the tension between needing to be wise and wanting to wash my hands of the situation, I wanted to escape. And yet there was no place far enough away to remove the knots in my stomach, the anxiety in my mind and the ache in my heart.

At home, Windsor and I clashed often. As her mother, I was the safest person for her to take her anger out on—and she did. Pushing me away with one hand and holding me tight with the other, she blamed me for all that was wrong and wanted me to make it all okay. It was a roller coaster of emotion and heartache.

When I told a pastor how much trouble we were having, much to my shock, he told me that Windsor was in rebellion and I should pack her bag, put it on my doorstep and lock the door. I could not do that nor could I agree with his assessment of my daughter. In spite of our rocky relationship, I held firmly to the idea that her anger came out of her deep woundedness: She had been hurt by her father's choices and she had been hurt by our divorce. She had many reasons to look for love in all the wrong places. I was not going to give her another one.

I love my daughter so deeply I can honestly say I was never ashamed of her, although I certainly grieved for her and with her. But there *were* times I could have strangled her!

WINDSOR'S STORY

The loss of my innocence and youth came with just two words: "You're pregnant." Little did I know that those words would take away, at the young age of 16, my life as I'd known it. The whole idea of it put me into an emotional spin. This is my story.

For a couple of weeks, I'd not been feeling well. I struggled to get out of bed in the morning and it was hard to keep my breakfast in my stomach. My gut told me "you're pregnant," but I delayed finding out for sure. Finally, with guilt and fear, I sat at the edge of my mother's bed crying, knowing I was probably pregnant and knowing my boyfriend was ending things.

"I think I'm pregnant," I blurted out, sobbing in shame.

> *Little did I know that the words "you're pregnant" would take away my life as I'd known it.*

My mother sighed. It represented all she wanted to say but could not put into words. She put her arms around me. For the first time in months, we both felt the same—neither of us wanted to face the reality yet. In fact, we spent the rest of the day trying to suspend any definitive action, trying to escape finding out the truth. Feeling the horrible possibility of pregnancy, we preferred the bliss of ignorance.

After school the next day, my mother mentioned a doctor's appointment she had scheduled for us that afternoon. Devastated,

I gave her dozens of reasons why we did not need to go. At first she understood and even sympathized. The initial struggle to face the reality of this situation was monumental for both of us. We both wanted to run away from it, pretend it had not happened to me or to our family. I gave my mother a hard time, but she finally managed to get me into the car. During the entire drive to the doctor's office, I was trying to convince myself I was not pregnant, thinking that because my family was who they are, God would protect them from this kind of situation. As we got nearer to the office, I began to curse myself and feel the blame for being in this predicament. I felt ashamed, confused, scared, lonely and stupid. I pleaded with my mother several times to turn the car around. I wanted to go home where I felt safe from the reality I was about to face. My mother did not have much to say. Something had changed in her. All of a sudden, I could feel her disappointment with me; our car became a box that had trapped me inside.

Mary's Story
(Another girl with a very different story, but the same issues)

I was scared, alone, thinking I was pregnant. On Valentine's Day, a good friend, an older woman, took me to get a pregnancy test. I was pregnant for sure. As I thought about telling my mother, I could see my life pass before me. She would not be happy. I was right. She physically attacked me and I had to go with my friend to her home. I hid from my mother and the rest of the family for over a month.

Abortion was the only option my mother saw for me. I was so scared, and not being sure who the father was, I felt she was right. After I returned home, my mother, afraid of what people would think, sent me to a maternity home in our state. I hated it, and after a week I moved north to stay with my aunt. She too thought I should have an abortion and she went so far as to get me an appointment for one.

Before this appointment, I was looking through my biology book and I looked up fetal development. When I saw pictures of a baby as old as mine, I cried. This was a person, a baby, and it was mine. I told everyone I wouldn't have an abortion, and again, my mother became very emotional. Everyone tried to reason with me, which meant getting me to see things their way. I wasn't about to change my mind. My aunt found a woman, Sara Dormon, in another state who was willing to take me in, counsel me and homeschool me until the baby came. So off I went again.

Note from Ruth: Sara helped both Windsor and me at a desperate time in our lives. Through her personal experiences and practical applications, underscored by her professional qualifications as a clinical psychologist, we knew we could trust her advice and counsel. Throughout the book, you can benefit from that same experience, advice and counsel by reading "Sara's Guidance."

SARA'S GUIDANCE

"I think I'm pregnant."

There are probably few things you will have to say or your parents will have to hear that will cause as much immediate and overwhelming anguish as those words. Most young women will in fact try to deny for as long as possible that they are pregnant. When you finally do confirm what you have suspected all along, your mother is usually the first one you want to tell, sometimes even before the baby's father.

After the tears, anger, hurt and just plain being scared, you must take action. You don't need to be told that you have choices and that abortion is one of them. In this country at this time, it is legal and is offered as a choice for young women with unplanned pregnancies. I'm not going to say that I think that is a good idea. I have counseled hundreds of young women who experienced a long-term, overwhelming sense of loss, grief and guilt after having an abortion. The experience may not be the same for all women, but it happens to so many that it overrides whether you believe abortion is right or wrong, whether it's "just getting rid of tissue" or killing a living child.

Your first two priorities are to find a doctor and a counselor. Taking care of yourself and your child should be the single most important thing on your list. This would include eating right, sleeping enough, exercising and taking your prenatal vitamins. Your child needs nourishment, and extra vitamins will keep you both healthy. With your body changing daily, you will find yourself very tired. You may also experience morning sickness, which may not be restricted to mornings. You need to listen to your body and take care of it because for the next months your body will be sustaining the life of another human being.

You need to find a good counselor who specializes in unplanned pregnancies. Choose someone you can trust, someone with whom you feel comfortable. If you don't feel comfortable with a counselor you visit, keep looking. For the next few months, this person is going to be your best friend and your worst nightmare, your confidant and your advocate. You may prefer this person to be a woman, or you may want your counselor to be a man, perhaps a pastor. You need to own your decision, so don't allow yourself to be told whom to choose.

Besides a trained counselor, you will need to have a support network around you of people you love and trust who are willing to walk beside you on this journey. As Mary's story illustrates, these people may not be family members. They will be some of your greatest assets on this journey. They will hold you, cry with you, keep you accountable and be your sounding board.

Sometimes they will just be present with you; sometimes that will be all you want. If the birthfather is part of the picture, he needs to be included in this circle. No matter how the two of you feel about each other, you have created a new life, for whom you are now responsible. For that reason, working together on the important decisions and developing a good relationship (for the time being) need to be important goals for the two of you.

> *No matter how out of control you might feel at times, you are in control of one thing: caring for this baby living inside you.*

There are so many things you need to know, but right now you won't be able to hear them all. Take this book and keep it near your bed. When you have a question or a concern or if you just need some reassurance that what you are feeling is normal, you will find something in this book for you. (*Nearly anything you feel will be considered normal.* No road map for your journey exists; everybody's journey looks and feels different.) So look forward with as much courage as you can muster, and hold on to the hands and hearts of friends. Your mother and father, the birthfather and your siblings will all find helpful sections in this book as well.

Try to remember, *No matter how out of control you might feel at times, you are in control of one thing: caring for this baby living inside you.*

You and the baby's father are responsible for your baby's conception and future. Accept advice and guidance from those you love and trust, but remember that, ultimately, the decisions are yours alone. You will want them to be decisions with which you can live.

With your vulnerability, heightened emotions and feelings of guilt, you may simply tend to comply with whomever is in authority, so as not to make waves. But this is your boat and your journey, so these are your waves. You will have to learn to sail some uncharted waters.

Recommendations

Birthmother

- Have your pregnancy confirmed by a doctor.
- Go to www.forpregnancyhelp.com and check out the Fetal Development link in the "Links to Related Sites" section.
- Tell your parents.
- Tell the birthfather.
- Get counseling.
- Make an appointment with a doctor.
- Have a meeting with the birthfather's parents.
- Remember:
    —Put the baby's needs first.
    —Rest and eat well.
    —Express your anger appropriately.
    —Maintain relationships with those who will be there for you.

Support Network

- Be supportive and compassionate.
- Encourage the birthmother and birthfather.
- Listen to them.
- Affirm the birthmother as a woman.
- Help the birthfather with his responsibilities.
- Get information from all sources.
- Be aware of the emotional roller coaster and try not to get on it.
- Remember your words have the power to heal and hurt.

Chapter 2

The Truth About Abortion

Sara

Probably no subject today is as polarizing as abortion. Everyone has a strong opinion on the subject. As I see it, people divide into four camps:

1. Those who feel abortion should be an option for all women at any stage of pregnancy
2. Those who feel abortion should be allowed, but they

themselves would never have one
3. Those who feel abortion is wrong except in cases of rape and incest
4. Those who feel abortion is wrong at any time for any reason

In defense of free speech, I would defend a person's right to hold any opinion. However, in this book, our intent is to persuade young women to refrain from making a decision about abortion until they have learned all they can about it.

Ruth and I both have what would be described as a personal relationship with Jesus. It would be very easy for us to say that we believe abortion is wrong simply because God says it is. While that is true, it is not persuasive to pregnant girls and it doesn't help anyone make a decision. Experience has taught me that when a young woman considers having an abortion, she is probably not particularly interested in what God has to say about anything. After all, God says that sexual intercourse is meant for marriage only, so His teachings on that subject have been already ignored by young women who find themselves pregnant but not married.

JUST THE FACTS

From a purely scientific standpoint—no God, no Bible, no judgment—here are some basic facts about how human life develops. They are true whether or not you believe life begins at conception:

- An egg and a sperm come together, and 7 days later they are implanted into the lining of the uterus
- 10 days—mother's period stops
- 18 days—heart begins to beat

- 21 days—pumps own blood through separate, closed circulatory system with own blood type
- 28 days—eye, ear and respiratory systems begin to form
- 42 days—brain waves recordable, skeleton complete, reflexes present
- 7 weeks—photos of thumb sucking
- 8 weeks—all body systems present
- 9 weeks—squints, swallows, moves tongue, makes fist
- 11 weeks—spontaneous breathing
- 12 weeks—weighs one ounce
- 16 weeks—genital organs clearly differentiated, grasps with hands, swims, kicks, turns somersaults
- 18 weeks—vocal cords work—can cry
- 20 weeks—has hair on head, weighs one pound, is 12 inches long[1]

Obviously, I could go on about fetal development, but I won't. The majority of abortions are completed within the first 20 weeks, and the point I am trying to make here is that from conception onward this is *not* merely a blob of protoplasm, a potential person, but a unique person with his or her own DNA and future.

Here's what Dr. Paul E. Rockwell observed:

Eleven years ago while giving an anesthetic for a ruptured ectopic pregnancy (at eight weeks gestation), I was handed what I believe was the smallest living human ever seen. The embryonic sac was intact and transparent. Within the sac was a tiny human male swimming extremely vigorously in the amniotic fluid, while attached to the wall of the umbilical cord. This tiny human was perfectly developed, with long, tapering fingers, feet and toes. It was almost transparent, as regards the skin, and the delicate arteries and veins were prominent to the ends of the fingers.[2]

When I make a decision, I want credible information on that topic. If I'm buying a car or choosing a college, a restaurant or a church, I ask someone who has had experience with that topic. So it should be with abortion, but it isn't always the case. Of course, even if you asked for information, people's opinions differ so much. I know women who have had abortions who still believe it is the best idea. There are others who have become crippled by the experience—emotionally, spiritually, psychologically or physically.

I do believe it's a much more important decision than is often portrayed, and that the best thing you can do is to educate yourself about fetal development and have an ultrasound so that you can see firsthand what is going on inside you.

> *Abortion brings an immediate solution to the problem, but it can also bring regret, remorse, guilt and a sense of loss.*

Abortions are legal in this country, and as long as they are, women will continue to have them. This decision, like the decision to have your child and to either parent or release for adoption, must be made after you have educated yourself about your decision. Young women considering abortion generally don't educate themselves as to the procedure. They want to believe what they are told, thereby alleviating the pain and, yes, some of the guilt. Abortion brings an immediate solution to the problem, but it can also bring regret, remorse, guilt and a sense of loss. Women who have those feelings after an abortion find that having made a conscious and legal decision (often encouraged to abort by those closest to them), they have no one to talk to. These are difficult feelings they didn't expect to have, feelings no one told them about. Why do they have these feelings? I believe the answer is because women were made by God to give life, not to take it away.

What Happens in an Abortion?

Besides hearing the statistics and the stories, women should know exactly what happens when an actual abortion takes place.

Abortions can be performed in a hospital or clinic. The woman can have a general or a local anesthetic. None of these procedures is pleasant to read about, but they all happen every day. There are three possible procedures:

1. **Suction abortion**—The doctor opens the cervix with long rods that become larger in diameter so that he or she has room to insert a suctioning device, which the doctor uses to suck out the baby and surrounding tissue.
2. **Dilation and curettage (D&C) abortion**—Placenta and other tissue are scraped out of the womb.
3. **Dilation and extraction (D&E) abortion**—The fetus is pulled out (often in pieces) with forceps as is the placenta and tissue.

Once the procedure is completed, the woman is given some time to recover, maybe an hour, and then she is sent on her way.

There will be some cramping and bleeding, but within a week, she will be back to normal. While this may not sound devastating, for many women it is, and it has long-term side effects for many of them.

SARA'S STORY

More than 30 years ago, I was one of these women. I found myself facing an unplanned pregnancy. I was on my own, living in Manhattan, holding down a good job and generally living the life of *Sex and the City*. Then one day I found out I was pregnant. While the baby's father and those for whom I worked would have supported any decision I made, I made the decision that was the easy way out. I have always loved children, but the timing was bad. Somewhere deep in my soul, I knew that it was wrong to abort the baby. I considered myself a Christian and I believed in the sanctity of life—unless, of course, it was going to complicate *my* life.

So I asked around and found a doctor who would perform the procedure. The baby's father gave me the money (which had to be cash), and off I went.

Now, as if I could outreach the hand of God, something happened as I was wheeled into the room for the procedure. The nurse looked at my chart and name and asked, "You wouldn't happen to know a Dr. Rice?" It turned out that this nurse had been in training at the same hospital with my father when he was a resident. What are the chances of that happening? It's as if the whole city were the size of my living room. The feelings I was trying so hard to ignore—fear, pain, shame and anger—all came pouring out. She walked over to my side and said, "Are you sure you want to do this?" My mouth said yes, but my heart screamed no!

Did I know what I was doing? Probably not in as much detail as I should have, but I felt as though I couldn't turn back. I had no plans for having this child, so I was trying to tell myself that whatever-it-was would be better off this way.

My memory of that day, March 2, is as clear to me as the days on which I later gave birth to my children. Having that abortion was the single biggest mistake of my life. Now I know that there are no unwanted children, only unwanted pregnancies.

Jennifer O'Neill is a friend of mine. At the age of 22, Jennifer starred in a movie, *The Summer of '42*. She was the model for Cover Girl makeup for 30 years, and she has had fame, fortune, beauty and what has appeared to be an idyllic, enviable life. Here is part of her story.

JENNIFER O'NEILL'S STORY

I was married at the age of 17, and by the time I was 19, after one miscarriage at 18, I had my daughter, who is now grown. She was very much desired and planned for. However, even though I had been a cover girl since the age of 15 and was well on my way to making over 30 films, I was not successful at marriage. By the age of 23, I was divorced and a single parent.

In the early '70s, I moved to New York City with my daughter to emotionally regroup after the devastation of my failed marriage. Although I was at the top of my career, to me, personal relationships, specifically having a stable partner, took priority. After a year of dating, I finally found someone wonderful. Craig was wealthy and powerful, and he treated me extremely well. He encouraged me as a person and didn't consider me just a pretty face. He was not yet divorced from his first wife, although they had separated years before.

When Craig proposed to me, I accepted with delight. Engaged and anticipating a wonderful future together, I moved in with him. Big mistake. I told Craig that I couldn't use any form of birth control for various (true) reasons, so if he wanted to avoid pregnancy, he'd have to be the one to use it. Another big mistake. Already a father of four, he said he did not want another child, but he also didn't try to prevent it. His behavior merely fed my hope of having a baby with him; I believed in my heart that he had reconsidered.

So when I did become pregnant, I was euphoric. I went straight from my gynecologist's office to my fiancé's opulent office suite in Manhattan, hoping he wasn't in the middle of some board meeting or conference call. It was only moments before he came down the hall and greeted me with an affectionate hug in front of everyone. I felt like a million bucks as he escorted me back to his office with a panoramic view of Manhattan.

I had asked my doctor to verify my pregnancy in writing, and I gave Craig the note. It seemed to take an eternity for him to examine that slip of paper. Finally, my future husband leveled me with a look that was contorted, foreign. "There will be no baby. You need to go get an abortion right away."

I was reeling. Hadn't we committed to spend the rest of our lives together in love? Craig's rejection of our child was his rejection of me as well. I sought out my parents for comfort and advice. But they also felt I should go along with him, rationalizing that I shouldn't bring a baby into the world that the father had rejected. "Besides," my mother added, "it's not even a baby yet; it's nothing. You can always try again later."

I went to my doctor the very next day, I must admit, hysterical. To my distress, he echoed my parents' words almost verbatim. "If the father does not want this pregnancy, then perhaps it's the wrong time. By the way"—then he told me the lie from the pit of hell that's still told today—"you're so early on that you're not even carrying a baby. It's just a blob of tissue at this stage, not yet an individual. If the timing is wrong with your pregnancy, there is always abortion. It's an extremely simple procedure." Surely this was a nightmare.

Although I remained with Craig in hopes that love would prevail—love for me and for our baby—the pressure by him to have an abortion only escalated over the next several weeks. I wish I could say that I prayed, but I didn't. I didn't have any faith in Christ then, so I didn't know God's truth concerning my baby, the life everyone else was simply calling "bad timing."

Finally, Craig threatened me in no uncertain terms. He said that if I chose to have the baby, he would take the child away and I would never see him or her again. He reminded me that he had the power and the financial wherewithal to bury me and my career. I knew I couldn't fight this man, whom I could hardly recognize by now. I caved in.

Craig made the appointment and, further, made sure I got there. He kept calling it an "appointment," but it was really an *abortion*, the end of our baby's life. He kept his arm around me as we walked into the waiting room. It probably looked like a gesture of love, but I knew it was to keep me from running away. I was inconsolable, crying until I had no more breath.

Even after I had been taken in for the procedure, I was crying so pathetically that the doctor went back out to see if Craig would change his mind. (This time, even through the fog of anesthesia, I noted that instead of referring to my baby as a blob of tissue, the doctor said, "You seem so intent on having this *child*.") But when he came back, he said he had never encountered anyone as sure about aborting a child as Craig was. There was no negotiation. The doctor went ahead. It was quick enough, as they had promised, although there was more pain than I had expected—certainly not more than I thought I deserved. I truly hated myself for having folded under pressure. My self-loathing would follow me for the next 25 years. I also erroneously believed that my multiple miscarriages following my abortion were somehow punishment for my heinous act of abortion, but the truth is God does not punish us like that. He loves us and wants us whole and healed in Christ.

When I walked out of that private Fifth Avenue office, Craig put me in a limousine and took me home to our penthouse apartment. Then he kissed me on the cheek and left for work downtown. I was left to deal with the death of our child, my dreams and our relationship. Needless to say, I moved out as soon as I could.

The years following were like walking through a soap opera. After several more failed marriages, five more miscarriages, bouts with alcohol and depression, and reproductive surgery, I finally had another baby, a son, in 1980. Then, after three more miscarriages, I had my last child, another son, in 1987. It was then that I finally turned to God at the age of 38 and found the security and forgiveness I had needed all along. God's restoration is truly amazing.

There are thousands of women who share the same pain Jennifer experienced. Regardless of your spiritual beliefs, the fact is that abortion is the ending of the life of your child, your grandchild, your niece or your nephew. If you know someone who is considering an abortion, please talk to her. Look in the back of this book for more resources to help her. Encourage her not to believe that abortion is the easy way out of her dilemma. Whatever you do, don't sit back and let it happen. God has a purpose for every life He creates (see Ps. 139).

Hunter Tylo is an actress and model, best known for her role for 12 years as Dr. Taylor Hayes in *The Bold and the Beautiful*. She more recently had her name in the papers for suing Aaron Spelling and Aaron Spelling Productions for firing her from a five-year contract on *Melrose Place* because she was pregnant and would not have an abortion. (Hunter won the case.)

Hunter Tylo's Story

After the birth of my first son, Christopher, I found myself pregnant again. Since my marriage had ended, I did not think I could take care of two children as a single mother. So I went to a clinic and a nurse there, whom I trusted, told me I was only carrying "10 weeks of tissue," and that it was not yet a child. I believed, because I wanted to, that having this done was really nothing more than forcing my period to begin. So like the unsuspecting tourist playing a shell game, I gambled away my child's right to live.

After the procedure I awoke to what seemed like hell. I was surrounded by sobbing women calling for their mothers. I hurt physically and emotionally. I had a feeling of deep loss and sorrow in my heart. I asked the nurse to show me what had been taken out and she asked me twice if I was sure I wanted to do that. I was sure. She then held up a tall jar. Through the fogginess of my condition, I saw what looked like thick strawberry jam and in it I saw a thin, transparent hand. That is an image I will never forget as long as I live.

After this, with the birth of each of my other children, I knew more and more clearly what I had done to end the life of each child's brother or sister. This experience has made me want to help expose the truth about sex and abortion. I want the truth to ring in the ears of all women!

Notes

1. *Abortionfacts.com.* http://www.abortionfacts.com (accessed July 19, 2004).
2. Dr. Paul E. Rockwell, quoted in Dr. J. C. Wilke, *Handbook on Abortion* (Cincinnati, OH: Hayes, 1975), p. 105.

Chapter 3

Who Cares?

Ruth

A mother, by definition, cares. Deeply. As Windsor's mother, I wanted to take care of it all for her; I wanted to hide her under my motherly wing! A mother cannot forget her child. There is no divorce from parenting—even if you might want one. Motherhood is for life. I made the commitment to Windsor on the day she was born—to be there for her, always.

I would be there to pick her up if she fell, but I had to let her fall and feel the pain of it. That made her think I did not care, which was double heartache for me. A birth-grandmother's own heart hurts while she watches her child's heart break, and she needs to manage wildly swinging emotions, including anger.

To show Windsor how much I cared, I listened and listened and listened some more. I heard things I did not want to hear. It was hurtful. Arguing was futile, but more often than not I fell into that trap. I tried not to break my daughter's confidences. She needed to be able to trust me with not only her angry outbursts but also her deepest thoughts and fears. I rarely let Windsor see my own anguish and doubts, which is one way I failed her.

Because I felt like a failure, I was tempted to try to make myself look better at my daughter's expense, to gain sympathy from others by playing the victim. I tried to steer away from that. I did not put her down or make jokes about her. I tried not to throw the situation back in her face and blame her for everything that went wrong.

Yes, she had upset my life—big time. It would never be the same. I felt she had embarrassed herself and my whole family. How could I hold my head up in church? In public? I just did it.

Birth-grandmothers come to understand, either through their faith or through counseling, that everyone makes mistakes and that mistakes do not have to be fatal. Some mistakes are just more visible than others. I learned that self-righteousness has no place in church, because the premise of the gospel is that we are all sinners. I learned not to let others define me or my child and never to sacrifice my child for my own reputation.

I was forced to take responsibility for my own issues. It was *my* anger. It was *my* doubt. It was *my* guilt and shame. As tempting as it was to blame someone else for them, I had to deal with them myself. By nature a nurturer and caregiver to the neglect of myself, eventually I needed counseling. It was not a one-shot deal—I had to confront my issues over and over because they had a way of showing up when I least expected them. I tried to keep short accounts. My feelings were uncomfortable. I did not like them, and I still don't.

To give Windsor a permanent record of my love and concern, I wrote her notes and letters. Words of love and concern can get

> *Words of love and concern can get lost in the shuffle, but a note, a card or a letter can be read and reread.*

lost in the shuffle, but a note, a card or a letter can be read and reread. Someone has said that to balance every negative word, we must receive seven positive ones. That may be why greeting card companies are in business.

JOURNALING

Journaling is a great way of releasing emotion and thinking through a problem. Flannery O'Connor said, "I don't know so well what I think until I see what I say."[1] If you have never journaled, get a notebook, date the page and begin to write. Write out the events and your thoughts and reactions to them. Write down quotes you come across that speak to your situation. The more you write, the better you will become at it. I have found that in the process of reflecting and journaling, God has met me in special ways, giving me insights and wisdom. Now is a good time to begin a journal, as an outlet for your thoughts more than as a record of pain and hurt.

While Windsor was going through this, I did not journal, and I regret that. At the time, I felt that by living through the pain and then by writing about it, I would be going through it twice, and I did not have enough energy for that.

Boundaries

Mothers can trust their instincts because they know their children better than anyone else does. When the pastor told me to treat Windsor as if she were in rebellion, I knew better. I knew she had just been trying to fill the hole left in her heart by her father's neglect, "looking for love in all the wrong places."

So I tried to be consistent, to set boundaries and then to stick to them. I wasn't always successful. But I knew boundaries could give security to both Windsor and me. With consistent boundaries, life at home could be a refuge for both of us. For us, good boundaries included rules about the friends she could socialize with, what time she needed to come or call home, keeping appointments and keeping up with schoolwork.

At times, Windsor felt that if she was old enough to have a baby and make decisions about its future, then she was old enough to make other decisions on her own, not realizing that there is a difference between age and maturity. My boundaries seemed to create conflict.

The Journey

Anyone involved with a child in an unplanned pregnancy becomes part of a complicated journey. Whoever shares the love ties is affected. Grandparents, siblings, aunts, uncles and friends are all gradually absorbed into the challenges and implications involved. This is too complex a journey to take alone.

I found others to lean on and told them what I needed. I allowed those I trusted to comfort me. I let them take care of me—to an extent. It was hard for me to ask for help and be on the receiving end. I am much more used to playing the role of being in control and taking care of others. I found a good counselor who helped me sort out my feelings and helped me make decisions that were best for Windsor, her child and me. I learned to ask myself, *What is best for Windsor and her baby?*

It was a bumpy ride and it often got messy. I felt like a pioneer hacking my way through a jungle of emotions and decisions. There were times I would have gladly given up or given in. But I knew that if I quit, it would be like writing across the sky, "I do not care." The implications of not caring and not taking care of myself would be far more disastrous. I would lose Windsor forever. My child's life and the life of her unborn child were eternal. My weariness felt eternal but I knew it was not. These relationships were far more important than what others might think, my shame and guilt, or my own desires.

By standing with Windsor, by caring, I knew I would not lose her. God had entrusted her to me. My ultimate concern for her was a spiritual one; I wanted her to know God's unconditional love and His forgiveness. I wanted her to believe that He could bring something good out of this.

WINDSOR'S STORY

Whether or not I felt my mother cared during this time is still a touchy subject. I now know that she was doing the best she knew how. When I got pregnant there were no instruction manuals about what to do for your pregnant teenaged daughter.

During my pregnancy I saw a mother who was trying to love me with her hands up, as if she were telling the traffic to stop. She was trying to teach me the lesson of tough love at a time when I just needed to be held. She didn't realize that the lesson she was trying to teach me wasn't nearly as tough as the one I was beating myself up over. I was dying inside; I was so disappointed in myself. In my mom's story she mentions getting counseling from pastors, friends and family, but she never came to me. I was 16 and pregnant; I did this on my own, so why couldn't she ask me what I thought we should do? Why did she exclude me from some of the biggest emotional decisions of my life?

If there is anything you take away from this book, I hope that it is this: A pregnant teenager doesn't need to be taught lessons of ridicule, shame or anger. The rest of the world is

> *My mother was trying to teach me the lesson of tough love at a time when I just needed to be held.*

already doing a good job with all of those things. Besides, the pregnant girl herself is already being hardest of all on herself.

CHERIE'S STORY

You may feel you are completely alone, just you and your baby. What you may not realize now is that your pregnancy will not affect you and your baby alone, but to some extent it will also affect your parents, siblings and extended relatives, as well as your baby's father's relatives. Your friends will also be impacted by your news. Some may be all excited and can't wait to go shopping and do the fun things that come along with a baby, while others may feel upset by your pregnancy and grow distant.

It is very important to have a good counselor. To this day I am in touch with mine, some 10 years after we met. Four different people gave Sara's name to my mother during the first week after

I told my parents I was pregnant. I don't think that was a coincidence—it was God. He put Sara in my life to help counsel me through my life's most difficult time and through my most important decision. She not only dealt with me, but she also spoke with my parents and met with my siblings, helping them with their feelings about my pregnancy and all it encompassed.

Again, my point is that your pregnancy not only affects you, but it also impacts your entire family in ways you may not see or imagine.

Once the confusion, excitement, turmoil and anger die down, there will be a few people left standing. These are the people who you will most likely have with you throughout this journey. You know they care, not because they say they do, but because they are there. Use them! Talk to them, listen to them, laugh and cry with them. Just remember, you are not alone, and these people care in the best way they know how, imperfect as it may be at times.

These people will have their own lives, jobs, school, friends and families. They are not pregnant. They are not facing the decisions you are. They are not consumed and overwhelmed by the situation. *You are!* Be patient with them—they are doing the best they can. This journey is uncharted territory for most people, including you, so don't expect too much or you will be continuously disappointed.

You must talk and tell people what you want them to know. Here's a good thing to remember: As much as you would like it to be different, people don't read minds. If you want them to know what and how you are feeling, you must tell them.

You will be amazed at all the people who do care. Before you tell anybody, you will have played out the worst-case scenario in your mind. Generally speaking, nothing will be as bad as you expect it to be. There may be parents, friends and your boyfriend whose reactions may be even worse than you expect, but they all eventually come around, once the dust settles. The longer you wait to tell people, the worse the scenario will get. Most people will handle it much better than you ever thought they would. They will be there for you no matter what. Give people the benefit of the doubt. Let them in and let them care for you. For those who overreact or react badly, give them time and space. I have never seen a parent, sibling or friend walk away for good.

I need to tell you that your friends will assure you that they will be there for you, to babysit or hang out, whatever you need. They mean it when they say it, but don't count on it happening, not for very long anyway. Most teenagers do not want to spend Saturday night babysitting for their friends, no matter how cute the baby is. They will go on with their lives, most of which will not include you. Your life has changed; theirs hasn't. As much as they want to show you they care, they really don't know how. Don't hold this against them. Again, tell them how you feel and how they can be there for you, if they choose to. If they don't, accept that too, and hang on to those who can.

SARA'S GUIDANCE

Surround yourself with people who care deeply about you and your unborn child. Be careful, though, because some of them who seem to share in the initial excitement will soon be gone. They just don't know how to act or what to say. Don't take it personally.

You don't need to be told that your parents care and that your mother cares very deeply; after all, she too is a mother. Their caring may, however, look different from what you had expected.

These very people who have said they care so much will do and say things that will irritate you, anger you, frustrate you and make you question just how much they do really care. What you need to understand is that caring about you and understanding what you are going through are not the same thing. Although

they love you, they have no idea what you are dealing with and they never will, unless they have had the same experience. Don't hold that against them. They are doing the best they can. Remember, they do love you and your unborn child.

Recommendations

Birthmother

- Listen to those you love and respect; you don't have to go through this alone, let others be there for you.
- Confide in your parents, they love you and care for you.
- Don't expect too much from too many.
- Realize your friends mean well, but don't count on them.
- Include the birthfather as much as he wants to be included.

Support Network

- Find a good counselor if you need one.
- Write the birthmother notes and letters to encourage and affirm her.
- Journal your thoughts and emotions.
- Be realistic in setting good boundaries; be consistent.
- Don't give up; be there for her.
- Listen, hug, laugh.

Note

1. *Letters of Flannery O'Connor,* "The Habit of Being" July 21, 1948, ed. Sally Fitzgerald (New York: The Noonday Press, Farrar, Straus & Giroux, 1979), p. 5.

The Decision Process

Ruth

The hardest decisions now forced themselves on us: Should Windsor keep her baby, or should we find adoptive parents? If she kept the baby, should she live with me? Was there room for her and the baby? How much was I willing to do? If I didn't think she could live with me, where would she live? How much would it cost? Did I have a family member who would take her in? A friend? Was she going to be covered under my medical

insurance as a dependent? Would the baby also be covered? What if there was a medical complication? Would she continue her education or get a job? What would happen when she resumed her social life? And long term, was I willing to help her raise her child?

First, I needed to decide what I could and could not do. Then I needed to inform Windsor and the birthfather, who was still deciding if he wanted to stay in the picture. My decisions would influence Windsor's decisions greatly.

To help with making so many decisions with far-reaching consequences, I found that I needed someone to talk to—someone wise and grounded. I chose to go to a local pastor to seek advice. He raised issues I hadn't thought of: the deeper questions of motivations, ego and spiritual components. He probed to find out if I thought God was calling me to raise the baby with Windsor. He counseled me to pray about what God would have me do.

My commonsense conviction was that Windsor was not ready to be a parent. And I knew that parenting wouldn't make her grow up. I wanted her to be able to finish high school unencumbered with responsibility for a child. When I took the pastor's counsel and prayed about it, I felt I could not take responsibility for Windsor's life and its consequences, but that she had to face those herself. I felt that stepping in and raising the baby in my home was not best for the baby, Windsor or me. I had to trust God with the results of my decision.

Once I made my decision, I wrote it down. I wrote down my reasons, any advice from others that resonated in my thinking, any Bible verse that seemed to confirm it for me. I knew that there would be many days when I would second-guess myself. I knew I would waver. (Sure enough, later I did ask myself, *Did I do the right thing?* If I hadn't written out the reasons why, I would have forgotten why I had made the decisions I made.)

I continued to rely on a small circle of advisers. They grounded me. I learned to turn a deaf ear to all the well-meaning folks who gave me their opinions.

CONFLICTS

My decision was not the one Windsor wanted me to make, and the struggle began. She accused me of avoiding my responsibility to her, of selfishness and abandonment. She tried her best to get me to change my mind. I was forced to love her with tough love, which is very hard.

Now it was her turn to confront the decision process. It was very difficult to sit back and watch, especially because I could see down the road to the ramifications of the decisions. I wanted to give her a crash course based on my hard-earned wisdom. But there is no use giving someone a crash course in wisdom. I had to let her make her decisions on her own. She did have options. If she wanted to keep the baby, I could give her legal emancipation so that she could more easily get a job and support herself and I would reduce my legal liability.

I found that the best way to help was to help her gather all the information I could get my hands on so that she could make the most informed decision possible. And, over and over, I told my daughter that I loved her.

As far as the present was concerned, I knew that Windsor could not live at home and continue with the same friends and activities. I didn't know of any families willing to take in young pregnant girls, so, eventually and reluctantly, I took Windsor to an out-of-state home for unwed mothers. This home seemed only too pleased to have Billy Graham's grandchild in their care. Windsor was terribly unhappy. It was not a happy match. She felt manipulated and trapped.

WINDSOR'S STORY

In my head, I didn't have to make a decision, because most of the time I was in denial about being pregnant. When reality hit me that I really was pregnant, I assumed I would keep the baby. I thought that way for a couple of months. When my mother made up her mind that she would have no part in helping me raise this baby, it forced me to think. Of course, I kept trying to change my mother's mind, but she wouldn't budge.

> *In my heart I already knew that I couldn't raise this baby alone, but I felt that if I admitted that, it would mean I had failed again.*

I had to ask the practical questions: What was I going to do? Where would I live? How would I support myself? In my heart I already knew that I couldn't raise this baby alone, but I felt that if I admitted that, it would mean I had failed again.

Every day there was an emotional battle going on inside of me. Every day I was torn between my desire to mother this baby and my desire to give my child a better life. I remember being very tired at this time in my pregnancy. Even lifting my arm was a chore in itself.

My mother and I were very much at odds with each other. Abandonment isn't a strong enough word to describe how I felt.

When she informed me of her decision to not help me with my child, I felt helplessly alone. It was a different kind of lonely, more like drowning where no one can hear you calling for help.

Just when I thought things couldn't get worse, my mother packed me in the car and drove me to an unwed mothers' home in Florida. Before we left, she said if I didn't like it, I could come home with her. But once we got there, the agreement no longer stood, and I no longer had the option of coming home. Again, my mother had made another big decision without my input, leaving me to live in that dreary home. (A couple of years later, my mother wrote that when she pulled away from the unwed mothers' home, she looked in her rearview mirror. She saw me with tears streaming down my face, but she resisted her desire to turn the car around and take me home. As I read that, tears filled my eyes again. I had to ask her, "Why didn't you?")

While I was in the home, adoption was shoved down my throat every minute of the day. The more they talked about it, the stronger I stood about keeping my baby. My roommate and I would discuss all the options. She was planning to keep her son, and she did do that. When we discussed adoption, she was not keen on it because she herself had been adopted, and she had the notion that her birthmother didn't care. We spent many nights staying up until 3:00 A.M. discussing our hurts, fears and options.

At that point, I had firmly decided to keep my baby. It wasn't until I was seven months pregnant that I began the real decision-making process. When I started to think about my options more realistically, it broke my heart. Either choice was hard. My father had offered to provide the baby and me a home. But since my father and I had our own deep relationship issues, it was never an option for me. In my mind I knew what was best for my baby, but try to explain that to your heart. It was a time of great turmoil. Just when I thought I had made a decision, I would change my mind.

This continued until 60 days after I gave my baby up, when the courts took away my rights. When Sara and I sat down and discussed what I wanted for my child, I had to be honest. What had I longed for all my life? What was the greatest heartache that I carried on a daily basis? It was the longing for an active father. I wanted my daughter to experience a daddy. I knew I didn't have a daddy for her. That one fact is what made up my mind to release my daughter for adoption.

Just a note: Like my mother, my father did the best he could. I can sit here and criticize everything he did, but he was my father for a long time. My father died seven years ago, yet there are still days when I wish he were here to take care of things.

CHERIE'S STORY

I was 17 when I got pregnant. My senior year of high school was supposed to be the best year of my life—and in a way it was because during that year I brought my son into the world. But in another way, this year was the hardest time of my life. I was going to go to college either way—whether or not I kept this baby—so I had to make two plans, one if I kept the baby and one if I did not.

I was unable to get welfare because I was 17 at the time, so there was no medical assistance to pay my prenatal bills. The bills were split between my parents and my boyfriend who was a college student with a part-time job. I had only a part-time job and no real money to speak of. I went ahead and applied to colleges, choosing schools that were close enough so that if I kept the baby, I would be within a reasonable distance to commute from home.

With the help of my counselor, I also planned how I would be able to raise the baby. I went to day-care centers and got prices. I went shopping and priced baby items—clothes and diapers, etc. I spoke with several other young mothers and tried to plan out how I would be able to go to school, work part-time and still have time and energy to spend with my child. I also tried to find any type of housing that would be available to my child and me. In my town, this kind of housing was basically nonexistent.

My parents made a list of rules for me, including how many hours a week they would babysit, when I could have company and how much they could help to support me, etc. Even today, when I look at this list, I still feel that it might have been a little strict, though I can now appreciate that they did it with the best interests of the baby in mind. Now I can also appreciate how hard it must have been for them to sit down and actually write the list. They wanted me to keep the baby, but they also were not in the position for my mom to quit her job to raise my kid. They were finished rearing their children, and they felt very strongly that this was my child and my responsibility. They were the grandparents, not the mom and dad.

Once I turned 18, I was finally eligible for medical assistance; I could get my prenatal visits paid for and receive other benefits. By the way, just because welfare is free doesn't mean that it is easy to get or that it comes without a hassle.

SARA'S GUIDANCE

The decision-making process is long, agonizing, painful and frustrating. Initially, you will do everything you can do to avoid making a decision, from denying the pregnancy to believing "Mr. Wonderful" will marry you so that you will all live happily ever after. (Unfortunately, you are the only one who is pregnant. More often than not, "Mr. Wonderful" will not be there for you, at least not in the ways you need him to be.)

I wish I could say there is a very straight path that everyone takes when faced with an unplanned pregnancy, but there is not. Every person is different, every situation is different, and all the people involved are different. People express emotions differently. This is a very emotional decision, and everyone around the birthmother needs to be prepared for an emotional roller coaster. The best advice I can give you here is that whatever emotions you have are normal. No matter how sure you are that you will not survive this experience, you will. You are a lot stronger than you think you are and as the saying goes, "What doesn't kill you will make you stronger."

Making an informed decision about either adoption or parenting involves solving problems well. As starkly objective as it seems, one of the best things to do is to sit down and answer the following questions:

- If I decide to keep my child, where will I live?
- Can I live with my parents?
- Can I live on my own?
- Can I live with the birthfather?
- If I decide to parent, how will I support my child and myself?
- If I decide to parent, how will I pay our medical expenses?
- Am I covered by my parents' insurance?
- Do I need to get medical assistance?

This is just the tip of the iceberg when it comes to the questions that need to be answered when you are deciding between parenting or adoption. Many of the questions do not have right or wrong answers since every situation is different and the people involved all have different agendas and needs.

Certain common threads run through nearly all unplanned pregnancies, and they are fairly constant regardless of the age of the birthmother, the involvement level of the birthfather or the educational background or socioeconomic level of those involved. One of the most common ones is the first reaction to the idea of adoption. Almost every young woman who ever has had the issue of adoption suggested to her will say, adamantly, "I could never do that!" Yet many of those same young women do eventually decide to release their babies for adoption.

You should make a list of pros and cons regarding both parenting and adoption. Even if the only reason you have for wanting to keep your child is because he or she is yours, that is reason enough. But is that what is best for your child? Your child's future well-being has to be your bottom-line focus.

Mother and Child

The mother of the birthmother must realize two very important things right at the beginning. First, she and her daughter are looking at this unplanned pregnancy from two *totally* different perspectives. The birthmother has no idea what to expect, while her mother is looking at this as a more mature woman who has given birth and raised a child. It is like two people holding an elephant—one holding the trunk and the other, the tail. They are holding the same animal, just from very different viewpoints. Second, the soon-to-be-grandmother must remember that she will use logic and reason to help her daughter make her decision. Her daughter will often have only emotion and anger to fuel her thoughts.

Many young women facing an unexpected pregnancy want to keep their baby in order to have someone to love who will love them back unconditionally. This is especially true with young women who do not have the support of the birthfather and who may not have a father present in the home. The people in the support network for such a young woman must continually bring her back around to the real issues at hand, which means that they will be subjected to her angry outbursts. Very often, the birthmother will be angry at everything and everyone, especially those who are supporting her, because she knows she can trust them to love her in spite of her anger.

If you are part of the support network, try very hard to overlook her behavior, and just love her. You do not need to excuse her behavior, but you should understand it, endure it and love her.

When you truly love someone as you love your child growing inside you right now, you want God's best for him or her, whether or not it includes you.

Birthmothers, if you can hear only one thing to help you through this decision-making process, it is this: When you truly love someone as you love your child growing inside you right now, you want God's best for him or her, whether or not it includes you. As hard as it may be to remember, you must realize that the person whose life is most affected by your decision is that of your unborn child. Think of your child's future. There is no right or wrong decision, only a decision that is best.

Adoption
As a birthmother, if you choose to release your child for adoption, your decision is both the most loving and the most excruciatingly painful decision you will ever make. You feel the tug-of-war

keenly. You are trying to make a win-win situation for all concerned, especially for the child.

If you have life goals and direction, as well as support from your family, you are more likely to see adoption as a positive thing that will enable you and your child each to have a chance to grow up, mature and achieve your potential. Girls who choose adoption see it as a good way to provide their child with a stable, two-parent family. This is especially true if the birthfather is not involved. Mothers know that children need a father.

Of course, even when you can make a list of 27 reasons why providing your child with a two-parent, financially stable, loving home is the best option, reason and logic tend to take a backseat to emotion. Your overriding reason to avoid adoption may be "because he or she is mine!" Again, please remember this: Your decision is to do what is best for your *child*, not for you, your parents, the birthfather or his parents. Your decision has to be made with the child's best interests at heart.

In addition, with adoption come legal issues of which you and your parents must become aware. This is addressed in more detail in chapter 16. For now, you need to know that if adoption is your choice, you must notify and involve the birthfather in order for it to take place. Regardless of whether you like it or not, he has all of the same legal rights and privileges as you do. (Often, naturally, the birthfather becomes persona non grata and the only emotion held for him is outright hostility.)

Parenting

Parenting is a viable and real choice for many women facing an unplanned pregnancy. Just as all parents before you have found out, there is no parenting manual that comes with new babies. Parenting is something you just do. For the most part, you will parent as you have been parented (unless you have made a conscious decision, as some do, to be the exact opposite of your parents). Parenting is a 24/7 job with no pay, long hours and little gratitude, but it can be done.

Keeping your child is not something you should consider lightly. Get as much input as possible from all the people you trust and respect. Talk to your parents. Talk to people whose parenting skills you admire. Ask them questions, and let them give you the benefit of their experience and wisdom.

To help you make the decision as to whether you should parent, seriously ask and answer the questions listed earlier in this chapter. You should price day care if you will need it, diapers, formula, clothes, cribs, doctors—anything and everything you can think of that you will need to provide a home for your child. The birth grandparents, yours and his, should put into writing what they will and will not be able to do to help you.

Your own plan should be in writing, too. Once you have finished it, go over it in detail with all those who have said they will be able to help you in any way. They need to know that you are serious and that you are going to be counting on them.

Ask yourself, *If I keep my child, where will I be and what will I be doing in five years?* Then ask, *What will I be doing in five years if I release my child for adoption?* Try to keep in mind that this small, helpless baby only stays that way for a brief time. Babies turn into toddlers and then into teenagers and adults.

No matter what your decision—adoption, parenting or abortion—only you can make it. You will have to live with your decision for the rest of your life, and most likely it will alter the rest of your life. Therefore, you should approach your decision with your eyes and mind open, not only to the present, but also to what the future will look like.

As much as we would like to offer you one clear-cut method for reaching your decision to parent or release for adoption, it doesn't exist. Everyone's journey is different.

Recommendations

Birthmother

- Realize your time is limited.
- Get counseling from someone who specializes in unplanned pregnancies.
- Include the birthfather in the process, if possible.
- Explore all possibilities.
- Understand there is no easy way out.
- Find out what your parents will and won't do for you.
- Make sure you have a way to pay for medical expenses.
- Base your decision on what is best for the baby, not on what you or anybody else wants.
- If you are comfortable praying, do it.

Support Network

- Make a list of what you will and won't do for the birthmother.
- Give the birthmother the benefits of your wisdom and experience.
- Accept that there is no right or wrong answer, only what is best for the baby.
- Be willing to accept decisions that are different from your preferences.
- Remember that you are not in control.

Finding the Perfect Family

Ruth

Things were not going well for Windsor. The home for unwed mothers where she was staying was not a good fit. I worried about this as I drove to Philadelphia. A friend in Philadelphia, Sara Dormon, had arranged a surprise birthday for two mutual friends and I was driving up from Virginia to be part of the surprise.

I have known these ladies for a long time. We get together several times a year to share our lives with one another—our concerns, feelings and thoughts about current affairs and books. We are all of different ages and backgrounds, but we have a deep bond that transcends our differences.

During the luncheon I confided in them about Windsor's situation. Sara, who often provided a home, counseling, advocacy and support for women with unplanned pregnancies, was able to ask me expert questions and give helpful suggestions. One of the women, who is very discerning, made the comment that Windsor's baby was going to be a special child and that God had His hand on it. I appreciated her words but did not think much more about them.

I drove home to Virginia feeling encouraged—until Windsor called to tell me how unhappy she was. She was homesick and miserable. If Windsor ain't happy, ain't nobody happy!

She was digging in her heels because she felt that the unwed mothers' home was "programming" her to release the baby for adoption. She resisted this and did not want anyone telling her what she should do—she was going to make her own decision!

Unbeknownst to me, my discerning friend had told Sara of a young couple in her church Bible-study group, the Connors, who had been unsuccessful in having a child. Sara suggested that they send a profile to her. They did, and she filed it away.

Good News

Later that week my phone rang and it was Sara on the other end, asking if I would consider sending Windsor to live with her. She and her family were willing to take Windsor into their home. Sara would homeschool her so that she would not lose academic ground. She would personally walk Windsor through the decision process of choosing between parenting and releasing so that Windsor could make the decision that was best for her baby. Sara knew far better than I all the issues and emotions involved.

As a tough lady with a tender heart for young women like Windsor, Sara would be a good match for Windsor. I could not believe the gift that was being offered so graciously. I didn't even pray about it! I knew this would be a good place for Windsor.

I called Windsor and told her about the offer. I think she saw this as a way out of the home for unwed mothers and as a chance to come back home. Initially, she wasn't committed to going to Philadelphia. I explained who Sara was and what the requirements would be, and, after many phone calls, Windsor agreed to meet her.

I drove Windsor to Philadelphia. While I knew this was the best possible solution, I had to let it be Windsor's decision or she would have resisted at every turn. However, I did tell her that we were out of options. In the end, she agreed to stay with the Dormons. I hated to drive away, leaving her in another new situation. How many changes had she already been through?

Decisions

Over the weeks, Sara walked Windsor through the realities of parenting and adoption. Windsor vacillated daily between parenting and releasing, testing every level of Sara's patience. She began to talk about adoption and wanted to look at Sara's files.

The file of prospective adoptive parents included the profile of the Connors. Once Windsor saw their picture and read their profile, she wanted to meet them. Joyce was a special-education teacher and Rob was a lawyer. Windsor felt an affinity for them because she had always had difficulty in school and had needed extra tutoring. And since she could argue the legs off a table, we had always teased her that she would make a good lawyer.

Sara made arrangements for the Connors to come to Philadelphia. I drove up from Virginia. I was nervous about meeting them. Would they like us? What do you say to someone interested in adopting your flesh and blood? What do you talk about? I am sure they were as nervous, maybe more so, than we were. I found them to be delightful and I liked them as people.

> *What do you say to someone interested in adopting your flesh and blood?*

I would have chosen them as friends and concluded that they were a stable and strong couple. If Windsor decided to release her baby to this couple, then they would be in our family but not of it. They would hold a unique and special place in our lives.

I was concerned about how they would respond to the fact that the baby they would adopt was Billy Graham's great-grandchild. Would it change things? I closely watched their reaction to the news. They didn't flinch.

Windsor asked Rob and Joyce many questions and told them that she was still undecided. We all needed time to come to terms with all the implications of such an agonizing decision.

WINDSOR'S STORY

I knew Sara had been working with another girl whose due date was a month before mine. Eventually we met. I was jealous of Cherie because she lived at home, she was still in school and the baby's father was still involved. Her life seemed to have been altered very little and that reminded me of all the people I felt had walked away from me. One day Cherie came over to go through profiles of couples. She had already made the decision to release her baby for adoption. Once she left, I asked Sara if I could look at the profiles. I think I was curious about these couples—what they looked like, what they did and why they couldn't have children of their own.

I remember as clearly as if it were yesterday. When I opened the files, I looked at the first two couples. But when I got to the third couple, I looked hard for some reason and read what they had to say. Staring at the picture, I told Sara that this would be the couple I would pick if I were going to give my baby up for adoption. He was a lawyer and I wanted to be a lawyer. She was a special-education teacher and I have learning difficulties. They were young, and he looked like he would be a wonderful dad. They presented themselves in such a way that they really stood out. Without even knowing it, I had just picked the parents for my child.

CHERIE'S STORY

I went through the whole process of looking for an adoptive couple for my baby. I started with a list of qualities that I felt were most important to me and that I could not bend on. When looking at different profiles of prospective adoptive couples, I have to admit I was a little discouraged. I met with several couples who did not fit the bill. Of course, it was easy to find something wrong with each couple. Why? Because they were not me, and I felt that no one else could be as good a parent as I would be. I wanted to find flaws in every couple so that I could say no good couple existed, and then I could say, "Oh, well, I guess I have to keep my baby"—even though I knew that would not be the best decision for my baby.

I had to realize that no couple will have everything.

SARA'S GUIDANCE

When you think about the family you want to raise your child, make a dream list (as long as you want) with all the qualities of the "perfect" family. You must first realize that even though you are seeking the "perfect" family for your child, there aren't any out there. There is however, a perfect family to love and rear your child.

> *I wanted to find flaws in every couple so that I could say, "Oh, well, I guess I have to keep my baby."*

On this list should be things such as whether you prefer a couple with other children; whether you want them to live in the city, suburbs or country; whether you prefer them to have pets; whether you want them to go to church; and whether you prefer an adoptive mother who works outside the home. Include anything that you feel is important. As you make this list, keep in mind the decision you are making will shape the rest of your child's life. It is an extremely important decision and should be made carefully.

The list is something you can do alone or with the birthfather if he is involved, but you should eventually discuss this list with your support network, especially your mother. She has been a parent and has raised a child, and she knows what is important. Once you have finished your list, go back and put a check mark beside those things that are nonnegotiable. Usually the single most important quality for you will be having a full-time, stay-at-home mom. This doesn't mean she will never leave the house until your child walks down the aisle, but it means your child will have a full-time mother for the most important years of his or her life. It means your child will not be put into day care so that his or her adoptive mother can fulfill her career goals. Incidentally, in my experience, women trying to adopt are more than ready to stay home and be full-time mothers.

Types of Adoption
Once you have your list, you need to decide what type of adoption will best meet your needs. There are open adoptions, and the degree of openness varies considerably. There are closed adoptions, which means you may or may not have a lot of say in the amount of information you receive about prospective families. The single most important thing for you to remember is that this is your child and your decision and that you are in control of the outcome. Obviously, the birthfather has the same rights you do, but he will usually go along with anything you want. This doesn't give you the right to be unreasonable in your requests; it just means that you have every right to express your wishes and desires and, if necessary, to negotiate with any prospective adoptive parents.

Open adoption. The majority of adoptions today are open. This means you will meet the prospective couples you are interested in considering as parents. You will be able to ask them questions, and they will ask questions of you. If you wish, they can be present at the birth.

They can and will be as involved as you want them to be. Once they have your child in their care, they will send you pictures, letters and may even make an occasional phone call. This goes on, in some cases, indefinitely. These issues are things you need to discuss with your counselor, parents and the birthfather.

Closed adoption. A closed adoption is just that, closed. You will not have the opportunity to choose the parents, you will know very little about them, and they in turn will know very little about you. After the adoption, contact will be minimal, possibly through another person, and there will be a lot of unanswered questions on both sides. Some young women do choose closed adoption, mostly as a means to pretend the whole experience has never happened. My personal and professional experience tells me this is not the healthiest approach. These girls who try to pretend nothing happened will need to talk about their painful experience, but if no one close to them knows what they have done, they have closed that door to healing.

Finding adoptive parents. There are several ways to find profiles of couples wanting to adopt. Couples can be found through an adoption agency, through an attorney or through an adoption facilitator. Adoption agencies can be found in the Yellow Pages, online or through recommendations. Attorneys who specialize in adoption can be found online through the American Academy of Adoption Attorneys. It is extremely important to have an attorney who knows adoption law, because it is a very complicated specialty and requires expertise. Adoption facilitators are not allowed in some states, so find out the laws of your state.

If you can, work with a facilitator for an open adoption, and you can look at as many profiles as you wish. You will look at profiles that most closely match the list of "perfect" family qualities you have written. These profiles are meant to tell you just enough about the couple to get you interested in wanting to know more about them. As an experienced facilitator, I recommend that you look at five or six. After narrowing the list to three or four, you can call to speak with your prospective families. Once you have talked to the couples, you will want to have a face-to-face meeting with some or all of them. Do this in a neutral place, like a restaurant. The birthfather should be invited to come if he wishes, as well as your parents, and possibly one other person. The prospective adoptive parents don't want to feel ganged up on, and you want your time with them to be as informative and relaxed as possible.

The goal of this meeting is to learn more about each other. Be prepared to be open. Ask questions and let them ask you questions as well. As much as you want to dislike them, try to at least be civil. It will most likely be at your first face-to-face meeting that you will begin to realize the magnitude of the decision you have made. Up to this point, there is a certain level of unreality to it. But now you are sitting across the table from two people who could be be taking your place in your child's life. Freely discuss what you want in the way of contact with them and your child. Admittedly, most birthmothers want pictures sent all the time, letters and the freedom to call at will. This will not be good for you, your child or the adopting parents. We would recommend that you ask for pictures every three months, including letters telling how your child is doing. All adopting parents are willing to do this, some even more. Things such as sending gifts, making phone calls and having visits with the child can be discussed as your relationship with the adopting parents develops. Each adopting couple is different; each birthmother is different, so there really isn't a fixed plan for this situation. Just remember, nobody can read your mind, so you must verbalize what you are feeling and what you want.

Choose parents that come closest to your ideal. It is entirely normal to find yourself thinking, *There is no one out there good enough to have my child.* As we said before, no one can love your child as you do, but there are people who can and will love your child, just not in the same way you do. You are that child's mother, now and forever. As you will someday find out, you can have more than one child and love them all, but your love is different for each child because all children are different.

Emotions

You will have many strong feelings at this time. Be assured that nearly anything you feel is all right. Don't let anyone tell you, "You shouldn't feel that way." You will have conflicting feelings. On the one hand, you will be grateful to the adopting parents; and on the other hand, you may hate them, especially the adoptive mother. She is taking your place, and you may hate her for it.

You do need to be careful of how you handle your emotions. Anger will only hurt you and your child. Try not to act out of anger, but do be aware you will feel it and that it is all right.

As I have said before, there are no perfect families or children, but you will do the very best you can to find the very best possible family for your child. Trust your instincts and your heart, and seek the advice of your support network. Your heart and your instincts will let you know which couple is best.

Recommendations

Birthmother

- Be realistic.
- Accept that no perfect family exists, and look for the best.
- Try to get to know the adoptive couple as people.
- Ask the adoptive parents to bring pictures of their families, homes, pets, etc., so you can see the environment in which your baby will be living.
- Make an effort to find some common ground with the couple.

Support Network

- Support the process.
- Support her decision.
- Support her.

Chapter 6

No Greater Love

Ruth

Although she changed her mind just about every hour (and that's normal), Windsor eventually decided to release her baby for adoption. It was a bumpy ride. She was on a roller coaster of emotion, vacillating to the very end, and it nearly drove me around the bend. I tried to stay steady and calm—at least on the outside! This was easier said than done, because Windsor pulled at my heartstrings and pushed all my buttons. I relied on my small circle of friends and my counselor to steady me. As I have said before, I wish I had journaled my thoughts more consistently, because it would have helped me sort out my own emotions and would have kept me more aware of my own insights and processing.

Like most women, especially mothers, I am a nurturer. I found that this was the time for me to nurture full throttle because my child needed me as never before. But she was more difficult than ever before. Impossible might be a better word. There were days I didn't want to face another decision, argument or emotion. I didn't want stamina; I wanted out.

To keep going, I needed to nurture myself. I did things I enjoyed. I love to go antiquing, so I did. I enjoy the beach, so I went. I read books for pleasure more than for self-improvement. I maintained the same goals. I was in school, trying to finish my college degree, and that kept my mind on things totally unrelated to what was happening around me. I exercised regularly and began to jog several times a week, which helped me feel better. I had trouble sleeping, so I asked my doctor for a mild medication. (There is nothing wrong in asking for such help when you need it.)

Despite my efforts, I became depressed. This was not my first bout with depression. It manifested itself not so much as a feeling of sadness but as a sense of weariness. It felt like I was walking through wet concrete. Deciding that it is not more spiritual to avoid medical help, I went to a doctor and asked to be evaluated for clinical depression. I received much help from wonderful doctors and counselors, which helped keep me from spiraling downward emotionally. I did not want my depression to get out of control. Others were depending on me.

Focusing on a creative project lifted my spirits and calmed my mind. I got busy making a quilt for the baby. Before my first child was born, I had made a gingham patchwork quilt and I had used it for each of my three children when they came home from the hospital. Now I decided to make one for Windsor's baby. This served several purposes: (1) It was a way of placing this child in our family, a symbolic way of saying to my daughter, "This child belongs to us," a very important message for Windsor to hear from me; (2) It was my special gift to this child, a gift that Windsor would be able to keep and use for any other children that might come later, thereby connecting her children to each other; and (3) It was also a fun project. It is very therapeutic to keep your hands busy when your emotions seem to be spinning out of control.

And would you believe that in the midst of all of this I got married! I wouldn't necessarily recommend doing something so important at a time like this! But I had already fallen in love with a kind man who also loved Windsor like a daughter. Since so much was going on in my life and we could not decide when it would be a good time to have a wedding, we eloped. I am amazed that he decided to take us on at this particular time. Windsor and her dad had a volatile and distant relationship. My new husband was loving but firm. We took good care of each other. We talked a lot. We dreamed about the future. We planned outings and had fun. We held each other often.

Empathy—a good exercise for me was to imagine how it might be for me if I were in Windsor's place: the shock and confusion of finding myself pregnant; the hurt and betrayal by the young man who had declared his love only to leave when I needed him most; the anger at everyone and everybody; the saying good-bye to my teenaged years while those around me were planning for the prom; and the effort to make decisions while coping with guilt and shame. It was a difficult exercise. I can hardly imagine the heartache of losing one of my children, especially the firstborn, to realize that he or she has only been loaned to me for a few hours, not mine to nurture. I wish I had written my thoughts in my journal and read them often so that they could have helped me empathize better with Windsor. As it was, I kept my imaginations in my heart.

GETTING READY TO RELEASE THE BABY

Time moved on, and Windsor began to focus on the process of releasing the baby. These decisions were hers alone to make. Even if I didn't agree with them, I knew I should support them. There were so many decisions: Who would be her Lamaze coach? Did she even want one? Who would be in the labor and delivery room? And, of course, who would be the adoptive parents for her child? If she asked for advice, I tried to keep it simple. If her decisions and reasoning seemed irrational to me, I told myself that was okay. She needed to make these decisions her way. I was not the one releasing my baby.

Windsor and her siblings had been dedicated to God when they were babies but not baptized. (I had reasoned that they would decide for themselves as they matured when baptism would be most significant for them in their spiritual journey.) One day, talking with Windsor by phone, she was discussing what sort of ceremony would be important as she released the baby. I mentioned the idea of her being baptized together with her baby. She liked the idea very much, so that is what we did. We contacted a Presbyterian pastor who had been our pastor when Windsor was a baby and who would be tender with all involved.

Windsor was ambivalent about the recommendation to have the adoptive mother present in the labor and delivery room, so she asked my advice. I thought it would be special for the adopting mother to see the baby born and also important for the baby in later years to know that both mothers had been there. While she agreed to some extent, Windsor was adamant that she did not want the adoptive mother to touch the baby first. This was more significant than I realized. As it turned out, after the baby had been born and put in the warming bed across the room, the adoptive mother happened to be standing in the way of Windsor's view of the baby, which agitated Windsor. I asked Windsor if the adopting mother could hold the baby and Windsor agreed. But she has regretted the timing ever since.

Issues that seemed inconsequential to me became monumental for Windsor. My job was to be supportive of her decisions. She had to decide what would give her comfort, not only now, but also in years to come.

WINDSOR'S STORY

Once I had made the decision to release my baby for adoption, I found myself in more turmoil than before. In some ways stating a plan provided a sense of relief, because I could focus preparations on that one choice. I no longer had to consider two big choices—just a bunch of little decisions that coincided with the one larger choice. On the other hand, admitting I was going to allow someone else to raise my child went against every natural emotion I had. Even though I had made a decision for adoption, I still went back and forth between the two options. One minute I was releasing and the next I was keeping. I knew in my heart what I would do in the end, but the woman within me didn't. I was knowingly about to put myself through a horrific experience; it wouldn't have been human not to try to fight my own intentions.

More than ever, I felt that I had failed not only myself and my family but also my baby. The reality of living without my own child began to sink in. I wouldn't know his or her first words. I would never be able to celebrate a birthday, provide comfort, help with homework. Every minute of the day was restless; the torture was endless. In trying to describe what it was like, I find that words aren't strong enough. My mom says that

I was impossible. I was impossible because there was so much conflict inside of me.

> *I knew in my heart what I would do in the end, but the woman within me didn't.*

The reason I decided to be baptized with my baby for the releasing ceremony is that I felt my short time with my child was going to be full of sadness and grief, and when I placed my baby in the arms of a loving couple, I wanted it to be a clean start on a new life—and I wanted that for myself also. When we left each other's company, we would have clean slates so that we could start new lives.

I decided to keep my new baby for four days. Even though my mom felt I was being irrational, I knew I needed those few days. I wavered on everything else, but I confidently stood my ground on this one thing. To everyone else, it seemed like unnecessary torture, but to me, it was my way of letting go. The only way I am going to make it through the rest of my life without her is because I memorized her every movement for those few days. I have never regretted that choice and am glad I stuck with it.

As my due date drew near, I was asked if I had considered having the adoptive mom in the delivery room. At first I would not hear of such a thing. I felt that was my private time to bond and I wanted to keep it sacred. However, the more I thought about it, the more clearly I realized that I wanted my son or daughter to have a unique story. I was most certainly different in every sense of the word, and I wanted my child to be special too. It seemed to me that allowing the adoptive mom to be present would make this story special. Because her adoptive mother was present at her birth, my daughter can hear her adoptive mom's recollections of the emotions she felt as she watched her being born, and she can tell her what my giving birth to her had meant. It meant I loved her more than myself. I wanted her more than anything else, but most of all I wanted the best for her.

There were a lot of decisions my mom, Sara, friends and family didn't agree with, but I stuck with my choices and to this day I have no regrets. My heart knew what I had to do in order to let go.

Tune in to your own heart and follow it no matter what. You only get one chance to let go. If you have regrets, it makes an already hard situation harder.

MARY'S STORY

I was 14, in the ninth grade, not sure who the father of my baby was and working for the first time in my life. My job was only at a fast-food restaurant and I was making just $5.25 an hour before taxes, but I was determined to keep my baby. I thought I could manage on my own, even though I had no place to live and no support from anyone in my family. I was too young to sign a contract for an apartment, but no one was going to talk me out of keeping my child. I felt this child would love me unconditionally, as no one ever had before.

My counselor encouraged me to at least think about the possibility of providing my child with a two-parent, stable, financially secure home, but my pride and my love for this child were getting in the way. More to humor my mother and my counselor than to actually find a home for my child, I looked at profiles of couples who wanted to adopt. To really look seriously would be admitting that I couldn't handle motherhood, and I wasn't ready for that yet. After a lot of talking, more crying and realizing that my fantasy was just that, I took a closer look at several couples. I liked two of them and wanted to meet them. I thought for sure I would like one more than the other, but I loved them both. Now I was faced with another hard decision: to which couple I should release my baby. After a couple of weeks, I finally decided on one of the couples and they had a party for me. I met all of their siblings, their parents, all of my baby's future cousins and everyone else who was special to them. I knew deep down inside I had made the right decision for my child, but it still hurt like hell.

SARA'S GUIDANCE

Well, you have decided that the most loving thing you can do for your child is to release him or her for adoption. You have taken the bravest, most courageous, most loving step a mother can take. The true mark of a mother is the ability to put the welfare of her child before her own. There is no greater love.

You will change your mind a hundred times before the actual birth takes place. And then, once you actually see and hold your baby you will assert to everyone within earshot, *"I can't do it! I can't give my baby up!"* That is exactly how you will feel. The mere thought of handing this beautiful little person over to someone else who will watch her grow, kiss her goodnight, see her first step and hear her first word—it produces an emotion so unbearably intense you really feel you will die if you have to do it.

Right up front you need to know that the adoption choice will bring you immediate, intense grief. It will dissipate, but it will never stop. On the other hand, although keeping the baby will mean less pain at first, you will develop a gradual ache that will grow in intensity until it is as painful as the grief of the birthmother who releases her baby for adoption. (This is because having a child to care for alters your life so drastically. You will experience the combined pain of a lost childhood, lost chances and lost opportunities. You might notice a growing resentment toward the child as you see your former life slip away. Even in a society in which more children have a single parent than two active parents, single mothers carry a heavy burden.) Either way, there is pain. You have chosen adoption and its immediate, intense pain that will diminish with time.

With all this pain ahead, your support network is crucial. You need them to remind you that you made the best decision for the right reasons—and what those reasons were. Especially from the moment of birth on, you will lose the ability to think rationally and logically. Hormones and emotions will drive you. You will be angry with everyone around you. Every fiber of your being will cry out: *"No! No! No!* I won't go through with it!" But somewhere inside, in the deepest place of your heart, you know that this same love that makes you say "No!" will not allow you

*You are now, and always will be,
the mother of your child.*

to change your decision. You will be able to release your child, and you will ultimately act out of that deeper love for your child's welfare. That is the kind of selfless, unconditional love and wisdom that comes with motherhood, and surely God gives extra love, mercy and grace to birthmothers who release their babies to adoptive parents.

Hold this truth in your heart: You are now, and always will be, the mother of your child. Nothing can or will change that, even the pain of relinquishment.

With this decision made, next you need to talk to your doctors to let them know you are planning to release your child for adoption. Tell them that you will keep them informed as your plans unfold. The reason for this is that some hospitals have rules as to how many people can be in the actual delivery room. They may require that you speak with the hospital social worker. These rules are meant for your benefit and protection.

You need a plan ready well before you go to the hospital, so you can feel a sense of control. Have a plan for the details of your hospital stay. Do you want the baby to room in? Do you want the experience of nursing your child? (Nursing, under these circumstances, offers no benefit to anyone involved and can really make the child's separation much harder than it needs to be.) Who, if anyone, do you want to visit you in the hospital during this time? Do you want the adoptive parents to come? Who will leave with the baby, you or them? Do you want a ceremony for the release of the baby? All of these questions need to be addressed now, before the baby arrives. Most adoptive parents are willing to cooperate with you, the birthmother, in any way possible, because they realize that you're making the ultimate sacrifice for their benefit.

After you tell your friends and family that you plan to release your baby for adoption, you will find that very few people will know what to say to you. This is especially true after you have had the baby. They don't know whether to be happy or sad, and of course neither do you. There really isn't a greeting card designed for women releasing their babies for adoption, although that should change!

The Adoption Option

One of the purposes of this book is to help put a new, less-threatening face on adoption. We want to make it as viable an option for young women facing an unplanned pregnancy as abortion or parenting. Approximately 120,000 babies are adopted in this country every year, although, at any given time, there are also more than 2 million couples trying to adopt a child. It's easy to see why so many couples travel outside the country to adopt. If even 10 percent of the 1.4 million women who have abortions every year would change their minds and carry their babies to term, releasing them for adoption, less than 10 percent of those trying to adopt would be able to become parents.

Choosing to release your baby for adoption can be a mature and loving thing to do, especially if you know you are not able to provide your child with the kind of life and home you want. It is never easy, never without pain, always an act of sacrificial love.

Recommendations

Birthmother

- Write down why you are releasing the baby for adoption and read it all the time.
- Keep a journal, writing to your child every day, using the name you have chosen.
- Make a list of the things you want to find in your adoptive family, have a list of questions for the family.
- Review profiles of potential families.
- Decide who should be present at the birth.
- Decide how long you want to spend with the baby after he or she is born.

- Try to prepare yourself for the release of the child.
- Consider a ceremony for releasing the child.

Support Network

- Affirm and support the decision for adoption.
- Listen.
- Nurture the birthmother and yourself—flowers and gifts are appropriate. Do things that you like doing.
- Rely on a counselor for help.
- Keep a journal, especially if you are the birth-grandmother.
- Help the birthmother prepare for delivery.
- Begin to focus on the future.
- Plan a special shower for the birthmother for after she releases the baby.

Chapter 7

Taking Care of Yourself

Ruth

In the previous chapter, I talked about practical ways I tried to take care of myself physically, emotionally and mentally. How did I take care of myself spiritually? Spiritual well-being is such a vital key to surviving a difficult time.

For many years I have made it a habit to read the devotional *Daily Light* every day and write down the verses that spoke to my heart on any particular day. I didn't stop when Windsor got pregnant. I needed it more than ever. I also kept a prayer diary. I recorded the things I was praying about for Windsor and her baby as well as for the others involved. Although it was my aim to do this each day, mostly my prayers were sporadic. But these familiar practices anchored me in very turbulent waters. It was good for me to keep routines when so much seemed to be out of control; they gave me a measure of stability.

Reading the Scriptures brought me great comfort. I loved reading the Psalms. King David wasn't afraid to speak his mind to God, yet he always came to a place of equilibrium where he could worship God with faith-filled perspective. The books of Job and Lamentations gave expression to the depths of sorrow that I was experiencing.

FORGIVENESS

One of the main issues I had to deal with was forgiveness: forgiveness for my daughter, forgiveness for others who had let us down, forgiveness of myself. I learned that forgiveness is a choice, a decision, and that it must be worked out in everyday events.

I dislike pie-in-the-sky, pat answers. I like to deal in reality. I resist the way forgiveness is often presented as a quick solution—just forgive! Forgiveness isn't quick. It is a decision that brings God to the wounds in our souls and begins the healing process. And it is a process. It takes time. We may take two steps forward and three steps back.

Forgiveness is like an unused muscle. When you start doing exercises to stretch a weak muscle, it feels so unnatural at first. If you remain committed and exercise daily in spite of soreness, soon you notice more flexibility and strength. You are able to move freely and find it hard to imagine a time when you didn't have the full use of that muscle.

Forgiveness is also like an inflatable clown toy that is weighted in the bottom. We punch it and it falls down, only to right itself again. Our emotions hit us hard—when we least expect it—and knock us over. But the choice to forgive will right us again.

Perhaps you are not particularly spiritual. Or perhaps you are very angry with God and would rather not deal with Him. Your daughter's pregnancy didn't take God by surprise. He sees the end from the beginning. Nothing you can do or say is new for God; He has seen and heard it all. He is bigger than your anger. You are going to need Him to help you make sense of all of this. Faith will transform your pain and loss. Faith doesn't make it easier, faith doesn't take it away, but you have Someone who will never leave you or forsake you. And He will strengthen you, guide you and even bring good out of your pain and loss. It helps to be in touch with the One who sees ahead because you will be in the dark most of the time! Now is as good a time as any to start to develop your spiritual side.

ANGER AND FORGIVENESS

My life had been altered by Windsor's bad choice. I did not expect it or want it, but here it was, dumped in my lap. Not only did people look askance at Windsor but also at me, her mother. I was mad about it, angry at these people, angry with Windsor, angry with the young man, angry with myself and with anyone else who happened to cross my path. My anger wasn't very rational. I wanted to lash out and frequently did, causing more damage. I was angry with myself for being angry. It was affecting my life, spiritually, emotionally and physically.

Anger needs to find someone to blame. I blamed Windsor's father. He had not been there for her as she grew up; he had rejected her early on as he became involved in adulterous affairs. He had left a huge void that she desperately wanted to fill. (The impact of a father's influence on young girls cannot be overstated. A father is key to a girl's self-image and self-confidence.) I felt that the church had let us down, and I was angry about that—why didn't they help us? I was angry with God. He had let me down—couldn't He have intervened? Anger—I had plenty to go around!

I just wanted it all to go away. I couldn't pretend it wasn't there, even if I did put on a pretty face and cover it with a smile. I was tired of working so hard to just maintain. I had often heard that the only one my anger hurt was me. Now I knew it to be true. So what was I going to do about it?

Unloading the anger began with forgiveness. I learned a lot from Lewis Smedes's book *Forgive and Forget: Healing the Hurts We Don't Deserve.* I made a conscious choice to forgive. I told God about my decision and asked for His help in carrying out that decision. It started slowly. The first day I had to remind myself of that decision 100 times. My anger flashed and unintended words slipped out.

Forgiveness is not a matter of "time heals" or of putting distance between you and the offender. It does not mean being blind or stupid or tolerant of bad behavior. Forgiving is not the same as forgetting. It is not denying reality or excusing sin or avoiding conflict or ignoring the consequences. Forgiveness looks the hurt straight in the eye, calls it for what it is and says to the offender, "I relinquish the right to make you pay. I give you the opportunity to make a new beginning." It costs you.

Forgiveness is not natural. Revenge is natural. Forgiveness is a God thing. And it is amazing to see what He does once we let Him into the situation through the gate of forgiveness.

So I made the choice to forgive. I said the words "I forgive you." My heart had been deeply wounded, and the healing process wasn't always smooth and pretty. My forgiveness muscle was stiff and sore. But in a strange way, the stiff unnaturalness of forgiveness served to remind me of my need all over again. The more I put my forgiveness muscle into practice, the greater my capacity for forgiveness became.

I learned that forgiveness isn't the same as reconciliation. Forgiveness is unconditional, and it can be one-sided, but reconciliation is conditional and it must involve both parties. Reconciliation requires repentance and changed behavior, sometimes over a long period of time to prove that it is real. Mere words don't cut it.

Asking forgiveness for my own offenses was the hardest and most humbling thing to do. It was tough. I needed to ask forgiveness of Windsor, my husband, God and others for my harshness, anger or whatever else my offense had been.

What if my daughter never asked for my forgiveness? What if she continued to hurt me with her choices? Even that couldn't stop me from making the decision to forgive every day. Each time I was reminded of what Windsor had done, I reactivated my decision to forgive. Forgiveness could only come from me. I saw it as a choice and a responsibility. I didn't wait for Windsor to ask for my forgiveness—I gave it. Once I had given it, I had done my part, and I stood ready whenever Windsor might ask (if ever). By choosing to forgive, it was as if I had made a large deposit in a heavenly bank account. Each time I needed to forgive anew, I could draw on that account.

It has taken Windsor and me years to uncover all the areas that have needed forgiveness. We try to address them as they come up, as God brings them to mind. It isn't easy. Recently we were up late talking. Windsor was telling me that she didn't think I had forgiven her. She was feeling that I had been keeping her out emotionally. I had been, and I told her why. She said that I had never told her that before and she asked my forgiveness. We both cried. Healing continues to occur.

WINDSOR'S STORY

The emotional pressure early in my pregnancy left me so overwhelmed, tired and depressed that all I could do to take care of myself was to sleep and take vitamins. I remember a time when my mother needed me to go somewhere and I told her I just needed to take a nap. My nap turned into a couple of hours. When she woke me up to tell me I needed to go, I informed her that moving my arm would take too much energy, so she allowed me to sleep and I slept through the night. I am grateful that my mother and my school schedule were flexible enough to allow me to get a lot of extra rest during this time.

After the first trimester of my pregnancy, my energy level increased and I started to be more physically active. I started participating in life instead of sleeping through it. Long afternoon walks not only allowed me to get fresh air but also helped me deal with depression. I found myself needing to be around people more and wanting to get involved in more activities. Whether it was making dinner, shopping, swimming or doing a puzzle, I wanted to participate in it. This was helpful, because 99 percent of the time my mind was occupied with thoughts of the baby, and this allowed me to focus on other things besides me.

During the second trimester, I began to focus on my emotions. Denial wasn't possible anymore because I was showing and feeling the precious life I carried. I began to look at my choices, listen to counsel and acknowledge my mistake. I don't mean that I didn't have moments in which I just couldn't believe I was pregnant, nor was I rational all the time, but I was starting to put my emotions in order and deal with them in a healthier manner.

I also focused on my family. Single-handedly, I had damaged my family. They no longer trusted me. I desperately wanted to change that, so one by one, I asked my family for forgiveness. They all said they would. It didn't cure anything, but it took some pressure off my shoulders and eased some of the pain I carried.

> *God seemed like my only friend—He was a source of great comfort during this, my loneliest time.*

I also found myself needing to reestablish my relationship with God. Before my pregnancy, my relationship with God had been nonexistent for a long time. Slowly, I started to pray more and read the Bible. My biggest comfort came from reading the book of Psalms, because one verse would be angry with God and the next would praise him. Psalms seemed to sum up how I felt inside. For the first time in my life, I began to ask spiritual questions and have conversations with my elders about what the Bible means. God seemed like my only friend— He was a source of great comfort during this, my loneliest time. Some of my biggest spiritual strides happened at this time.

CHERIE'S STORY

I felt so emotionally drained and up and down that I did not know how I was going to make it through. As if life and pregnancy were not difficult enough, an unplanned pregnancy with a huge decision to make is even harder. You contemplate the rest of your life—either as a parent to this child or as a birthmother without your child.

It's important that you take care of yourself. Get prenatal care. Take your vitamins. It's amazing what I could do for my child that I wouldn't do for myself. I remember eating right, walking daily—all this just for my baby. I loved him so much, and I wanted the best for him that my needs became secondary.

Spiritually—I felt very guilty for having sinned and for doing what I had done. It's not like I was sleeping around and didn't know who the father was. I had been in a relationship for some time, but we had been out of God's boundaries of blessings—yet not out of God's thoughts and love. A sin is a sin; my boyfriend's and my hidden sin was now public. I know God has forgiven me, and I have learned to forgive myself. This was not the end of the world though it seemed that way at times. God promises He will never leave us or forsake us. Jesus died on the cross so that sins like these would be forgiven. His forgiveness doesn't give us the right to continue living contrary to His boundaries.

I felt like I had let my parents down big-time, and I wanted their forgiveness. My pregnancy also made me very appreciative of my parents and all they had done for me. Faced with the possibility of raising this child alone, I was so grateful that they had not thrown me out or forced me to get an abortion. I thanked them for giving me the option of having a choice, for not saying "this is what you are gonna do—final answer." Once I saw how expensive and time-consuming and all it means to have a child, I was so grateful that they were there for me and supportive.

I remember going to church and just sitting there crying every time a child was dedicated. I was wondering, *Is this going to be me here with my child next year? Will I be up there all alone—a single mom? Or will this dedication be going on somewhere else, and I won't even have a clue that it is happening in some faraway town where my child will live with his new family?* It was very hard to go to church anyway, because already I was so full of guilt and all the emotion that comes with pregnancy.

SARA'S GUIDANCE

The physical, emotional and spiritual care you give yourself and your child is very important. This is, to say the least, a very stressful time, and stress affects us at levels we don't even realize.

Because your baby will feel the same emotions you feel, try, as much as you are able, to minimize the stress. When babies hear what is going on around them, even though they can't understand the words, they can feel the tension and hear the volume. It is a good idea and practice to allow others in your support network to help you where they are able. You do not have to do everything yourself. Allowing others to help you makes them feel as if

Do things that you enjoy: read, walk, listen to music, shop, whatever helps you relax.

they are making a tangible contribution to your life and the life of your child. Don't be afraid to ask for fear it will make you seem dependent and needy. You are, and that is okay for now.

If you are smoking, drinking, doing drugs or having unprotected sex, *stop, stop, stop and stop!* Now it is time to think of your child's welfare. At least one of these things got you into this situation.

Exercise is a good way to reduce the stress in your life and to make your pregnancy and delivery easier. It will keep your body in better shape and it will make it much easier for you to get back to your prepregnancy weight. Remember, you are not training for the Olympics; you are taking care of yourself and your baby. Be sure to get your doctor's permission before you start an exercise routine.

Talking to the people in your support network is also good for stress relief. Often you don't want guidance—you just need someone to talk to. Do things that you enjoy: read, walk, listen to music, shop, whatever helps you relax. Your baby will benefit and so will you.

Write to Your Child

Every birthmother is concerned about the possible negative messages she may be sending to her child. You don't want your child to think you chose adoption because you were selfish, didn't love him or her, or just didn't want the bother of a child. One way to be sure your child will know the truth is to get a blank-paged book and begin to write to your child.

You can even choose a boy's or girl's name if you know the gender of your baby. Start with "Dear Sara" or "Dear David," and tell your child exactly how you feel. Write about yourself, the father, the grandparents, aunts and uncles. Explain how and why you made the decision to release him or her for adoption; tell him or her about how you selected the adoptive parents. This journal is something you will give to the adoptive parents; so if you want to have it for yourself later, be sure to make a copy. Of course, you also can type it on a computer.

These are your words, your feelings and your emotions for your child to read after he or she is old enough to ask questions and understand the answers. You won't leave any significant questions unanswered and, most important, you will not be relying on the adoptive parents to speak for you. Adopted children tell me that being able to know what their mother (and father) went through would have made all the difference in the world to them growing up. These feelings have absolutely nothing to do with their adoptive parents as much as they have to do with natural, human curiosity.

Think Ahead

It is also a good idea to make or buy some sort of tangible gift such as a blanket, a collage of pictures, or anything else that will someday have special meaning for your child. This will be a connection between you and your child, something your child will always have to prove how very much you loved him or her.

Mentally, you also need to begin to prepare for the actual birth. You need to take birthing classes, have a birth coach, and decide whom you do and do not want to be present at the birth. Decide if you want the birth videotaped and if yes, by whom. You are in charge, and you need to be very clear about what you do and don't want. The one person you will most likely want with you during childbirth is your mother. But remember, you and she are not looking through the same set of eyes or feeling from the same heart. It isn't that she doesn't want to understand what you are going through. She can't. If she says something stupid or insensitive, forgive her. She is your mother, and she loves you.

As much as you would like to ignore the spiritual side of this dilemma, you cannot and should not. Regardless of your religion or lack of it, the life growing inside of you was created by God. As hard as it is to believe, God loves this child more than any human ever could. God's love is eternal. You may feel anger toward God for letting you get pregnant. But the truth is that you and the birthfather made you get pregnant. Naturally, you will feel shame for being an unwed mother, but someday you will realize that there are many worse things that could happen to you.

You may feel as though you have done something that God can't forgive; you haven't. God loves you deeply and passionately. He will forgive you, and if you ask him, He will personally help you through this experience and all experiences yet to come. Even though you may not feel forgiven (and you probably won't feel any different), try to live as if you are. The hardest part will be forgiving yourself. Remember, if the creator of the universe can forgive you, you should, someday, be able to forgive yourself.

Recommendations

Birthmother

- Write to your baby.
- Talk.
- Make things to send with your baby.
- Read things that feed your soul.
- Keep on with your life goals; if you don't have any, make some.
- Physically take care of yourself and your baby.

Support Network

- Listen.
- Make things to send with the baby.
- Take care of yourself; you can't give away what you don't have.
- Encourage the birthmother to keep her goals.

Chapter 8

No One Can Love My Baby as Much as I Do

Ruth

My daughter spent nine months thinking of very little else but the baby within her, who became literally the heart of her heart. She loved this child more than anything. This little person, who had walked each step of the way with her, filled a hole in her heart that nothing else could occupy.

I spent the same nine months thinking about both Windsor and the baby. My heart was divided. Because Windsor had decided to release her baby for adoption, I felt I could not afford to become too attached or to give my heart away. This was a matter of great consternation to Windsor. She accused me of not loving her child. Of course, I did and do love her. That little girl is my first grandchild.

> *I longed to see her grow up, to hear her laugh and to hear her call me "Grandma."*

But she was loaned to us for only a few hours. I held her only a few times. I longed to see her grow up, to hear her laugh and to hear her call me "Grandma." There is a unique ache in my heart that does not go away, a lump in my throat that arises at odd moments. There are times I think I have "gotten over it," and then the pain comes again. I am not sure one ever gets over it.

Life doesn't prepare us for this. The pain of birth-grandmothers may be worse because we have walked the path longer. We can see down the road to the grief of separation, the heartache of loss, the agony of self-doubt. We have our own grief to bear as we watch our daughters grieve and struggle. We know the peculiar heartache of watching our daughters' heart break—repeatedly. Our role is just to be there, no longer able to shield them from the realities of loss and grief. We have to let God do His work in their lives during this time. If we step in and try to control things, we may hinder His work.

We birth-grandmothers play a special role. We will watch our daughters give away the one thing they cherish most in all of their young lives. They have sacrificed their health and their reputation by carrying the baby to term. They have walked through the valley of the shadow of death by giving birth. They have not withheld their love for the one they cannot keep, and yet they take the unimaginable step of giving that most precious loved one to the waiting arms of another woman.

These young birthmothers think no one can ever love that baby as much as they do. They are correct. Adoptive mothers do not know those depths, and they will never be called on to give up their own flesh and blood voluntarily.

I have never sacrificed as much as Windsor has. I admire her courage. She knows this now, but back then she did not think I cared, because I kept so many of my emotions to myself. In retrospect, I should have let Windsor see more of my feelings. I held back because I was afraid of coming unraveled. I felt Windsor needed me to be strong. In reality, she needed me to feel her feelings and to share mine.

WINDSOR'S STORY

When I first met the adoptive couple to whom I was going to release my child, I remember thinking that Rob was awesome and would be a great dad but that Joyce was just okay and would be an average mom. It wasn't because she wasn't as fabulous as Rob—it was because she was the "other woman." Joyce would rear my daughter, hold her, talk to her, listen to her secrets and love her up close. I was jealous and angry that this woman was going to be my daughter's mother. What had she done so right to be the chosen one? I felt somehow less qualified to be a mother if

I said that she was fully able to be my daughter's mother. She could never be me, and I didn't want to believe she could love my daughter as well as I could.

I distanced myself from Joyce, not allowing myself to know her beyond a certain point. I wanted to feel justified in not liking her. I maintained my distance and jealousy for years. The distance didn't exist because of her lack of effort but mine. Ironically, I trusted her and liked her enough to give her the one thing that was most precious to me, but still in my mind she was the "other woman."

After I gave birth, I was still lying there when Joyce went over to my baby. I wanted to yell, "Get the hell away from my daughter! Who do you think you are?" I didn't yell. But I watched her be the first to touch my daughter. Probably her emotions couldn't be contained and she just had to touch her. But I felt she had just ruined my special moment. I was so angry that I wouldn't let her visit us again at the hospital. When I was discharged, I told everyone that she couldn't be near us, that this was my time with the baby and she just needed to let us be alone. Everyone thought this was cruel; to some extent I knew I was being cruel.

I tried to do the best thing in spite of the way I felt. When I walked into the house, I made a slow climb up the stairs with my baby in my arms. I knocked on the door with tears streaming down my face. When Joyce opened the door, she seemed surprised to see me standing there. I handed her the baby and said, "Here is your daughter." Boy, did those simple words and actions feel like a knife slicing through my heart and soul. But I knew that my daughter and her mom needed that time together too.

CHERIE'S STORY

When Nancy, the adoptive mother, came to the hospital after my son was born, she came into the room and asked to hold him. I just about threw up when she held him and put her pinky finger in his mouth. How dare she touch my baby? It made me so mad to see her holding him. I just wanted her to go away. This was *my* time, our family time with our baby. It took all of me to let her in there, but I knew that she needed to see him and bond with him right then, as he was only a few hours old.

I look back now and think, *Duh, this is the person that you are trusting to be this child's mother for the rest of his life, and you can't let her hold him?*

As hard as it is, I think girls need to see adoptive parents with the baby. After all, they are soon to be that child's parents. I know of other girls who did not let the adoptive mother hold the baby or who made a big stink over it. I feel they should have realized that the adoptive parents needed to be with the baby too.

Nevertheless, I feel very strongly that the birthmother needs to spend time with her child. It's hard to know how much time is too much in terms of getting overly attached and making the letting go more difficult than it already is. There is no set time. For me, it was very important that I got to spend time with my son and my boyfriend alone, just the three of us. Our little family—even if it was all a fairy tale—it was nice to be together. It was also important to me that my parents spent time with the baby and that my siblings came to be with him as well.

My son was with me for several days before he could legally leave the state. I felt I did not want to bring him home with me because it certainly would be harder to let him go, and I would have memories of him in the house and in my room. We had a ceremony the night he left. My family, my boyfriend's family and the adoptive parents were present. A minister prayed, and we all shared and passed him around. It was the hardest thing I have ever done, walking out that night without him. But God got me through it, and I knew that this was the best decision for my son. So what if my heart had been ripped out and I thought I would die. I did heal, and I am thankful my son is alive and thriving in his home with his family.

I think naming your baby is important, although you must understand that your baby that you gave birth to is now their child, and they can name the baby whatever they please. We chose a few names and told the adoptive parents that we would be honored if they would even consider naming him one of the names we had chosen—either as a first or middle name. I understood that he was their son now, though, and they could name him whatever they chose. In the first year or so after he was born, it was hard to hear him called by the name they had given him, "Jesse." In my mind, he was Isaiah. But in all the letters and conversations, his name was Jesse. After a little over a year, I began to accept what they had named him. He answers to the name Jesse. He does not know the name I gave him at birth. Accepting that was a big step. I figured I had better get over it and accept the fact that there was nothing I could do to change it. I think it also helped me to accept a little more that he is *their* son. He will always be my child, but they are his parents and he is their son. Our son.

SARA'S GUIDANCE

"No one can love my baby as much as I do." You won't get any arguments on this statement. Everyone else in your child's future will love him or her in a different way. Yours is a unique relationship. From the moment you find out you are pregnant to the moment of birth, your baby becomes a part of you in every way—physically, emotionally, mentally and spiritually.

You will give your child a name, even though you may never say it out loud. You are this child's mother in every way except the one that matters the most to you right now—taking your bundle of joy home from the hospital and living happily ever after. Your decision to release your child is based on the fact that you are not able to provide the happily ever after.

Keep telling yourself that your decision to release your child for adoption was made in the best interests of this child. Remind yourself that there is no greater love than to give your child the best possible life, even though it doesn't include you. Remember also that you (and the birthfather) have had an active role in determining who the parents of your child will be. Sometimes the rest of us wish we had had the opportunity to choose our parents.

> *You have become, at a great cost, a member of a very special group of women—birthmothers.*

Your love for your child is the most selfless love on Earth. It transcends what most people will never understand. You have become, at a great cost, a member of a very special group of women—birthmothers. From this day forward, you will always be your child's mother, no matter what. It is true, no one will ever love your child as much as you do. You have proven your love by your willingness to endure the pain and the heartache of allowing another woman to have this child. You are doing this *because* of your love. This is the type of love for which there are no adjectives besides mother love.

One important thing you can do to tangibly make this child your own is to obtain an original birth certificate. This will have the name you have given your child, and it will list you and the birthfather as the parents. You will fill out the form at the hospital, and the birth certificate will be mailed to you after you go home. The adoptive parents will get another birth certificate when the adoption becomes final, months down the road. But the original birth certificate will be yours forever.

Recommendations

Birthmother

- Keep writing to your baby (the birthfather can do this too, if he wants to).
- Accept that others can and will love your baby, although their love will not be the same as yours.
- Allow others to love you and your baby.
- Give the baby a name and get your baby's birth certificate.

Support Network

- Listen to the birthmother.
- Have outside friends and counselors who will listen to you.
- Don't be afraid to show her your emotions.
- Allow the new child room in your heart.
- Birth-grandmothers: Verbalize to your daughter your admiration and your emotions.
- Birth-grandfathers: Be there for your daughter—share what you feel.

Chapter 9

Letting Go

Ruth

Windsor's plan for releasing the baby was clear: She wanted to take the baby home from the hospital for four days before she released the baby to the Connors. I was not sure it was wise. I knew as a mother that it would make the release so much more heart-wrenching, but it was Windsor's decision.

Even so, in the hospital Windsor kept vacillating between wanting to keep the baby and deciding to release her. It was a tortured time, made worse by the fact that her hormones were out of whack from childbirth. Her emotions were all over the place. We all kept reminding her why she had made the decision to release, calling her back to her reasons.

Upon Windsor's discharge from the hospital, we took the baby to Sara's home. I watched my daughter's joy for four days while she held her infant daughter and learned to diaper, feed, rock and play. This baby girl of hers was beautiful; Windsor had produced something perfect.

Our family gathered to be introduced to the newborn. She was part of us and nestled herself in our hearts. When Windsor had decided to release her baby, I had wanted to protect my heart by holding back from bonding with her. That proved to be impossible; this child moved right in and made herself at home in my heart. Although the time was short, it was wonderful.

But our joy turned to anxiety and dread as the day of her release approached. It was like waiting for death—I found myself counting down the days, then hours.

The lawyer came over to have the final release papers signed. The Connors took care of the baby in the den while we looked at the papers in the dining room. The intensity of Windsor's struggle was written all over her face. She cried. She sat staring at the papers. She begged me once again to let her bring her daughter home and help raise her. She blamed me for her dilemma and was angry with me. I was angry that she was putting me in this position. I reminded her of the reasons she was releasing her baby. I could not push; I could only wait until she was ready. After a long time, she signed the papers.

I wonder if a governor feels the same way as he signs a death sentence for a convicted man.

THE RELEASE

As we drove to a friend's house for the baptism service and release, tears poured down my cheeks. My heart was breaking, not only for the loss of the baby, but also for Windsor. The pain was so intense that I was not sure I would make it and I felt that my heart would simply burst. I wanted to run. I wanted to be anywhere else, do anything else but this. And yet, of course, I wanted to be right there with my daughter.

At the baptism service, Windsor looked beautiful, dressed in pink. Her face was Madonna-like as she cradled her baby close. Her eyes were pools of unspeakable sadness. After the baptisms, we took photographs, passing the baby to each family member. Those photographs reveal so much love and so much pain.

I was not prepared to watch her devastation. Windsor's heart had been broken when the young man had walked out of her life. Now it was shattering again as she released the most important thing in her life. It was agonizing to see her pain, although I couldn't fully enter into it. None of us could help her carry it, nor could we protect her from it. All I managed at that moment was to observe my child in agony while experiencing my own.

I said, "It is time." Windsor held the baby that much closer. She smiled bravely for one last photograph with her child. Her eyes, swollen from crying, her heart breaking, she whispered "I love you" and gently, ever so gently, placed her baby in the waiting arms of the adoptive parents. They got in their car, weeping as they drove away. Watching them through the window, Windsor wailed as a mother who has lost her first and only child.

Going Home

We said hurried good-byes and got into our car to head to Virginia and home. Spent in grief, Windsor slept.

I was exhausted emotionally and physically. I felt as if I were coming apart at the seams. How would we go on? Our lives had been changed forever. I was weary of trying to be wise and gentle and everything for everybody. I had nothing left to give. My husband took over. He was focused and strong; we found security in his strength. He didn't say anything as we drove home, but he held my hand and let me weep. I caught him looking in the rearview mirror more than once as he checked on sleeping Windsor.

When she awoke, he engaged her in lighthearted conversation that was focused on the near future. He answered her questions honestly and assured her that he would be there for her in the weeks and months to come. He asked her about plans to go to the beach and if she wanted to go hiking with him. He included her in all of our outings.

> *You need to hold your daughter, to put your arms around her. Tell her you love her and do special things with her.*

He showed us his love in actions more than in words. When advice was called for, he offered it with clarity and gentleness. When decisions had to be made, he was focused but considerate. When our emotions were raw, he was tender. When boundaries were needed, he was consistent but loving. He was sympathetic but never lost perspective. He let us cry and made us laugh. He let us vent but held us tight. I will be forever grateful for his gentle, kind strength.

Let me say to birth-grandfathers, you are important to the process. You provide stability. You need to hold your daughter, to put your arms around her. Tell her you love her and do special things with her. Do not shut her out. It will be awkward for you, but you are a very important part of the picture. Don't walk away from her tears. Don't just buy her things—give of yourself. What you do and how you do it can make the difference in how well your daughter puts her life back together. And while you are at it, hold your wife; listen to her.

Windsor came home with an empty womb, an empty heart and empty arms. She faced hours, days, months, years—a lifetime—with part of her heart missing. Windsor was only 16, and her friends were just learning to drive while she was learning to live without her baby. This was real grief. A death had taken place in our family and now we had to cope.

The retelling of our story is painful. I know that we made the best possible decision for the baby, and I have never regretted it. But without a doubt, this day was one of the worst days of my life.

WINDSOR'S STORY

I insisted that I keep my daughter for four days after I was released from the hospital. In order to let go, I had to take in everything I could about her. I wanted to see her sleep, cry and be still. I needed to capture her smell and watch her every movement. At the time, I didn't really understand why I insisted on having that time, but now I know that it was my motherly instincts. I knew I couldn't survive this ordeal if I didn't absorb her. I wanted to know every detail of my daughter before saying good-bye.

As time ticked away, I became very anxious and agitated. I wouldn't let anyone else hold the baby for very long. I wanted to make time stand still.

But before I knew it, the third day arrived and the lawyer needed me to sign—it seemed to me—my life away. As I held my daughter and I tried to sign papers and keep my emotions under control all at the same time, I finally realized that I had to put my daughter down in order to complete the task at hand, so I took her out of the room and asked if the Connors (Rob and Joyce) would hold her. After I came back to the table, I sat there for a long time, hoping my mother would change her mind and say, "Come live with me." She never did, and my delay could go on no longer. With tears streaming down my face and the worst pain I had ever felt, I signed the papers. It was just a taste of what was to come.

July 29 is forever etched in my heart. I can remember every moment, every glance and every emotion as if it were happening to me right now. Earlier in the day, my mother convinced me to leave the house to go get my hair done. I went, but I just wanted to get back to be with my baby. Most of the day went more quickly than I wanted it to. The dreaded end was so close I could see it.

My family packed my car with all of my stuff as I got ready in a pretty pink suit and put my daughter, Victoria, in a white dress my sister and I had worn as babies. The time had come; we needed to get in the car and go to where we were going to have the ceremony. I stalled and stole a few extra minutes alone. I was consumed by unbearable pain. Words fail me in trying to describe what it felt like; there are no words strong enough to describe that kind of pain.

I managed to place the baby in her car seat and buckle myself in. On the drive to the ceremony I began to unravel, no longer able to keep my emotions all contained inside. Tears streamed down my face. Without a word being said, my mom knew what was happening in the backseat—my heart was being ripped from my chest inch by inch. It was like being tortured. I wanted to take my baby and run. I didn't want to go through with the adoption, because I was in too much pain.

I sat beside my daughter, stroking her face. My heart just couldn't understand my reasons for doing this. To the end, this was going to be a fight; this was so unnatural. I wanted to remember her every facial movement, even though I could hardly see her through my tears. Outside, the day was warm and sunny, but to me it was dark and foreboding.

My immediate family gathered around. Victoria and I were baptized by a pastor friend. I don't remember a word he said. I was too busy holding and watching my little girl. Once the ceremony was over, we took a lot of pictures with everyone.

Then the nightmare took a turn for the worse. Mom gently reminded me it was time to go. The air in the room was heavy. No one knew what to do except sit there and watch in horror. Sara asked everyone but a select few to leave. I let only a few people stay. It was just too heart-wrenching and it had to be private. Once everyone left, we took the last pictures. I changed my daughter's diaper and then she quickly fell asleep. I begged and prayed that God would allow me to see her eyes one more time. My mom reminded me again that it was time to go. I begged my daughter to open her eyes and this time she did. I told her, "I love you and we will meet again." As my heart broke in two, I took Victoria to Rob and Joyce, who were experiencing their own joy and pain. I gently placed her into the arms of the loving couple I had handpicked for her. They held her, hugged me and cried.

It seems that only seconds went by before they were in the car leaving. I had arranged this detail—her leaving first. I knew I couldn't leave her behind. She had to leave first, or I would have gone back for her. I remember watching them get in the car, running to the car and staring into their window. I watched them pull out of the parking lot and drive away. Then I collapsed on the ground. I couldn't take any more. I just wailed. With my heart torn out, I got into my mother's car for the long drive home. The nightmare had passed; the worst part was over; now I could curl up and sleep.

When I got up the next morning at home, I felt as if something horrible had happened, but it was over. I didn't wake up sobbing, screaming or terribly upset. My body had gone numb. I could openly talk about everything with few tears. I went to the store to have my pictures developed. Being 17 and needing to get out, I went on a long drive. It seemed as if I was okay. I went about my business, happy to be home.

The end of August came, and I returned as a senior to my high school. Amazingly, I continued on the right track, continuing my daily walk with God, hanging out with my parents instead of going out on the town and getting involved in many activities. However, six weeks after my daughter was born, I suddenly began to feel again, and the pain that had been there all along unleashed itself upon me. All hell broke loose. This girl who had been living a peaceful life seemed to be consumed by chaos. I felt as if I was being attacked on every side and all I could do was run in circles trying to escape. I did everything and anything to ease the pain, but it had a hold and wasn't going to let go.

SARA'S GUIDANCE

A birthmother wrote the following poem after releasing her baby:

Wish upon a star and your wish may come true.
I wished on a star and they came to take you
away from my arms, but never my heart;
together nine months, we are now far apart.
Don't ever think that I didn't care.
I love you, I miss you, in spirit I am there.
And when you are ready, by your side I'll be,
Together again, my baby and me.

Having just read this part of Windsor's story, you may want to back off on your decision to proceed with adoption. I would be surprised if you didn't. You are facing one of the most emotionally wrenching experiences you will ever have to handle.

You have wrestled with the emotions of your heart and the logic in your head, and this wrestling will continue up to and beyond the point of your child's birth and release. At times, your emotions will overcome you like a tsunami and you will feel as though you are drowning. Perhaps drowning would be a welcome relief from this knifelike pain that is cutting your soul and heart to shreds. You can expect that much of your emotion will come out as rage directed at anyone or anything handy. This is normal. However, don't lose sight of the fact that you are in this position because of your own choices and no one else's. I say this because you will want to blame everyone else, especially the baby's father, for your pain.

When, where and how do you want to release your child to the adoptive parents? There are as many ways to go about this as there are young women doing it. Again, these are your decisions to make because this is your child. You don't need to make this decision alone. (If the birthfather is involved, of course he should help.) But yours is the final word.

Perhaps you have decided that the less time you spend with your child the easier letting go will be. But if you end up changing your mind when the time actually comes to do it, say so. This is your child. I think you realize that spending a lot of time with your baby will make the release harder, but you may be willing to accept the pain in exchange for more time. Just don't expect the people around you to read your mind. You will have to tell them what you want.

Legal paperwork. As you read in Windsor's experience, the lawyer will bring papers that will begin the process to terminate your parental rights. This is a very difficult experience. There will be other papers to sign that allow your child to be able to find you when he or she turns 18. This process varies by state, which is another reason you should have an adoption attorney advise you, especially if you are a minor. All of this will have to happen after the baby is born—when you are already an emotional basket case. Be sure you have someone with you when you sign these papers. The attorney should be able to bring the paperwork to your home or wherever you are living. Remember, you can ask for what you want. There is no preordained time for this to be done, but it shouldn't be put off too long.

Release ceremony. In my extensive experience with young mothers releasing their children to adoptive parents, even those birthmothers who have no strong religious background usually want to have some kind of ceremony. Some of them want to be baptized along with their child; others want everyone involved praying over the child. The releasing ceremony should happen in a place that is somewhat neutral without being impersonal. It is extremely important for you to be in a safe place and with people with whom you feel safe. If you have a church home, that can be a good choice. Do remember that you are going to have to walk into that church again. For this reason, you should use a room that you would not normally use and an entrance that you won't have to use again. You will relive this time again and again, so it is best to find a place you don't visit often.

Most important, take pictures, even videocassettes if it doesn't seem too intrusive, so you can always have pictures to keep. You may want to give your baby a blanket or something saved from your own infancy. Virtually anything you want to do, within reason, is all right.

Take care of yourself. If you decide to keep the baby with you for a few days, you will not want to sleep. You will want to just hold your baby, watch him or her sleeping and do whatever you can to have as much time with your baby as possible. This too is both normal and understandable, but without sleep, when the time arrives to release him or her, your hormones and emotions will be so shot you won't be able to function. If necessary, take something to help you relax and sleep. Please try to keep in mind that this entire process is emotionally draining for all involved, so it is important to do whatever you can to take care of yourself.

> *I gently placed my daughter into the arms of the loving couple I had handpicked for her.*

I know it hurts to even read the term "letting go." Rather than focusing on the negative aspect of letting go, try to remember that you are doing the most loving thing possible for your child, which you have determined is the best possible decision for him or her. You are living out what it means to be a mother.

It may be helpful to actually say good-bye out loud while holding your baby (or anytime). It's okay to cry with your baby and to let your child hear your voice. The best time to give your child the letter or journal you have been writing is at the time you release your child to the adoptive parents. This may be the only message your son or daughter will ever have from you, and it will be very important to him or her.

Grief. When you release your baby for adoption, you're going to experience the kind of loss and sadness a mother feels when a baby dies. You may also find yourself experiencing a sense of relief that your decision has been made, your pregnancy completed and your life can get back on track. Please remember that almost any feeling you have in the days following the separation from your child will be normal. Grief is a necessary part of this experience and critical to the healing process. Even though you are sure you made the best decision for your child, it hurts. Hurting is okay.

Remember that your body is not only grieving, but it is also working to return to an unpregnant state. You have a lot of hormonal changes, weight changes and general body changes happening. Organs that were displaced by the baby are back in their original places, and you can finally sleep on your stomach again. You don't have to go to the bathroom every 10 minutes, and now you can get out of a chair without the assistance of three large men. Any soreness from pregnancy or the birth will be going away and your milk-filled breasts are returning to their prepregnancy size. It is just as important now to take good care of yourself. If you get run down physically, you will get run down emotionally, which will make you more run down physically, which will let you get more run down emotionally, and so on and so on and so on.

You have physically let go of your child, and yet your baby will live in your heart and mind forever. No matter how much time passes, thinking of your child will always bring a tear-filled smile. Hopefully you will have pictures and letters to document your child's growing up. And then someday, when and if your child is ready, you will meet again.

Recommendations

Birthmother

- Try to be prepared for one of the most painful, difficult, life-altering events you will ever experience.
- Keep focusing on why you are doing this.

- Plan a meaningful, life-honoring ceremony.
- Plan to bring your journal and any gifts you have for the baby.

Support Network

- Keep your focus on what's best for the future of the child and the birthparents.
- Be there for them in every way possible.
- Acknowledge your own grief, and allow yourself to take the time to grieve.
- Acknowledge what the birthmother has done out of love for her child, and honor her.

Chapter 10

Moving On

Ruth

After the release of your child or grandchild, you will grieve. It is truly like a death. For months your world has revolved around this child and now everything is behind you. How do you move on? How do you pick up the pieces?

Slowly, one piece at a time.

I found comfort in the Scriptures. I read Isaiah 51, "[I] will look with compassion on all her ruins" (v. 3). "Ruins" imply failure, plans gone wrong, a wasted landscape with bits and pieces scattered around. Imagine God's look of love and tenderness as He surveys our ruins. Did you realize that, even when our lives and hearts are a wasted landscape and all we can see are bits and pieces, God's gaze does not condemn or blame us? He sees hope where others see failure. He binds up the brokenhearted. He specializes in restoration and in building a future—a good future. He restores the ruins in order to rebuild our hearts as His dwelling place.

HEARTS MEND SLOWLY

Windsor and I reminisced. We looked at pictures. Our hearts mended slowly, and the process was up and down.

Some days after I thought the grieving was over, I was surprised to have it triggered when I least expected it. Once I was scheduled to speak at a ladies' luncheon in the city where Windsor's baby's adoptive grandmother lives. It did not cross my mind that she might attend the luncheon until I was getting dressed the morning of the event. My stomach tightened and tears filled my eyes. My emotions caught me off guard. Moments like this are normal in the process of recovering from grief. It takes time and cannot be rushed.

Each person recovers in unique ways. Windsor needed me to cry with her, but I tended to carry my grief inside. She got upset with me because I did not show my grief in the same way she did. Some say sorrow is halved when shared. Perhaps it is. But I felt the pain was just too great to share with anyone but God. I was trying to achieve some sense of order in the midst of the messiness of grief. Whether or not it's the best way to deal with it, I deal with loss by getting busy doing something, to get my mind off it. Windsor read my behavior as uncaring. I couldn't behave any differently, especially not after more than nine months of bearing up under her anger and confusion. Now, without neglecting her, I had to survive my own sorrow and move on.

And I still remember. Starting on my granddaughter's first Christmas, each year I send a gift in her name to a charity that cares for children. Without being intrusive in her life or that of her new family, it gives me a way to remember her and a way to let her know that her birth-grandmother remembers her.

RESTORATION

You may have heard the saying, "Failure does not have to be final." We can have hope in God's ability to restore. To me, living fully means living in double reality, knowing my pain and doubt but also knowing God's love. He has not abandoned me in a time of trouble or left me to merely muddle through somehow. He is *with* me.

The Scriptures tell us over and over again that He will give us the strength we need. He is with us in the midst of our heartaches. He knows all about what we are feeling. He has walked that same road. Jesus not only experienced life here on Earth in all its agony, but He also became what we are, human, so that He could understand fully and comfort us in our need. He knows what it is to be an outcast, to be rejected, humiliated. He knows physical pain, emotional torment and mental anguish. He has wept over His children. He knows what it is to grieve. In Him, I found—and continue to find—the comfort and strength I need.

When all the questions have been asked and all the answers examined; after all the pain and loss, self-doubt, guilt, hurt and anger; when I have exhausted myself in the asking, arguing and demanding; I quiet myself and remember what King David said in Psalm 131, "I do not concern myself with great matters or things too wonderful [difficult] for me. But I have stilled and quieted my soul; like a weaned child with its mother, like a weaned child is my soul within me. . . . [I] hope in the LORD both now and forevermore" (vv. 1-3).

Now I can say, with Jean Valjean in the musical version of *Les Misérables*:

My soul belongs to God, I know,
I made that bargain long ago.
He gave me hope when hope was gone.
He gave me strength to journey on.[1]

CHERIE'S STORY

Moving on is hard to do, but as you get busier, time will pass quickly. If you take it day by day, you will be surprised how fast the time passes.

For the first year, I remembered every month on the twenty-first: I would think, *Today he is three months old*, or *Today he is six months old*. I'd think of how, in some ways, it seemed like just yesterday that I had been at the hospital having that baby, yet in other ways it seemed so long ago that I had held him in my arms.

I was planning on meeting with my son's father every year on the actual birthday for dinner, but that has yet to happen. Every year around his birthday, I get a little emotional. People call and e-mail me just to say, "Hey, we remember, and we think you made a great decision and did a brave thing." It's nice to know that people care, and that, yes, they still remember.

I have fewer pictures of my son up now than I did years ago. It's not that I want to forget—how can I? But for me it's easier not to walk by the same picture of him every day and think about him. I like to think of him and pray for him when he comes to mind.

You may decide not to tell everybody about your child, especially as you get older and farther away from the actual adoption.

Some people just don't need to know. Some may even judge you and not take the time to understand. When people ask if I have kids, I answer that question differently depending on who is asking. I find it's just easier not to get into it and bring up feelings that go along with it. If a person stays in my life and I feel that person needs to know, then I will tell him or her when I feel that the time is right.

Sara's Guidance

As you begin the grieving process, you won't want to move on and you won't want anyone else to move on either. You'd prefer to wallow in your misery. Your emotions will behave erratically. You won't think you have a reason even to get out of bed, let alone get dressed and leave the house. Remember, as you go through this, those around you are not able to understand what you are feeling, not even your mother. Don't get angry at them for not being able to feel your pain.

Relief will come as you begin to realize you have made the most loving, courageous and best possible decision for your child. Allow yourself to feel the pain of the loss. Grieve in whatever way you need to, regardless of what others say. Recall the tender moments you had with your child and allow yourself to cry. Do not allow anyone to tell you to "get over it and move on." You will never completely get over it. But you will move on. Just do it at your pace, not the pace others expect.

Perhaps you're stuck on the idea that you are damaged goods, that no man on Earth will ever want to marry you, and that you might as well just pack up and go to the convent now. This is a good time to remind you and your parents of the importance of counseling. Talking with a counselor or a support group will help you rebuild your self-image. Look for a birth-mother support group. It will be enormously helpful for you to be able to talk to someone who has had this same experience, someone who can look you in the eyes and heart and say, "I know exactly what you are going through." Ask your counselor or the adoption agency to help you find such a group.

Set some goals for yourself. Finish high school; go to college; get a job. Whatever you decide, planning for the future will help you to heal faster. It will help you to realize your experience has not been in vain. Make your child proud of you. Even if you don't feel like moving on for yourself, do it for your child.

Cherie, whom we have heard from throughout this book, went on to college after she released her son. This past year her son celebrated his ninth birthday. Cherie currently works for a major insurance company.

> *Even if you don't feel like moving on for yourself, do it for your child.*

Start a new journal at this time. It will give you the chance to put those feelings, emotions and thoughts about your new life into perspective. In addition to writing, some women want to have a permanent and visible reminder of their child. They plant a tree, a shrub or a bed of flowers that will bloom every year.

Talking to friends is also an important part of this grieving and healing process. Of course, some people will listen for a while and then they may pull away. It isn't that they don't care; they just don't know what to do to help you.

You will never, ever forget that child you carried beneath your heart for nine months, and no one is asking you to do so. (But you will be glad you moved on with your life if you and your child meet again sometime down the road.) Concentrate on your goals and your future. The more you do this, the faster you will begin to heal.

You have been through one of the most difficult circumstances of your life. You have learned new things about yourself and you have found out you are much stronger than you thought you were. You have discovered what unconditional love looks and feels like. You will never forget your child or what you have learned. You have been able to handle experiences you didn't know existed before, and you have matured beyond your years. Take it all and use it to make yourself, your family and your child proud of you.

Recommendations

Birthmother

- Continue counseling.
- Pursue your goals.
- Make a living memorial.
- Express your hurt and anger in good ways.
- Don't let others tell you how you should feel.
- Talk and remember.
- Continue journaling.
- Keep a scrapbook of your adoptive parents' photos, letters and updates.

- Make your child proud of you.
- Forgive yourself.
- Be proud of yourself.

Support Network

- Listen.
- Remember.
- Talk.
- Support the birthmother's goals.
- Express your pride in her.
- Weave this experience into the fabric of the rest of your life.
- Live in forgiveness for yourselves, the birthmother and the birthfather.
- Don't berate yourself.

Note

1. Herbert Kretzmer, *Les Misérables*, Hal Leonard Corporation.

Chapter 11

I Don't Fit In

Ruth

After all this, how do you move on with your life and fit back in with your friends? How do you relate to them? To your family? To people in your church? This was more uncharted territory for us.

We arrived back in Virginia at loose ends, not knowing where to begin. What do you do the day after you release a child for adoption? I wanted to get my life back to normal, but it never would be. My emotions were spent and I was exhausted. A piece of my heart was missing.

I felt that my daughter needed me to provide a sense of routine. The world had not come to an end and there were things that needed to be done. There were groceries to buy, meals to cook, mail to catch up on and phone calls to return. I thought that doing these familiar things would bring some order back into our lives, but Windsor resented me for plunging into them.

A few of my female friends gave Windsor a shower. By doing this, they were not ignoring or condoning what had happened—they were affirming Windsor. They gave her a luncheon and presented her with gifts for herself. Interested in seeing the pictures of the baby and letting her tell her story, they asked questions about her future plans and ideas. It was a lovely thing for them to do, and I will be forever grateful.

Many others, perhaps most, did not know what to say or do, and they did not inquire as to what would be appropriate. They assumed that doing nothing is better than doing the wrong thing. Of course, we interpreted their silence negatively.

Then there were the ones who happened to have daughters who had not gotten pregnant. When they asked about Windsor, I cannot describe my guilt, self-condemnation and shame. They didn't intend to make me feel like a failure, but they did. I felt that the word "failure" had been tattooed on my forehead for all to see.

Where was the church? Church friends didn't do much better. Not knowing what to say, they too remained silent. When my church friends tried to help, my raw emotions and fragile self-esteem felt as if they had been trampled by combat boots. They offered pat answers and "help" that was conditional. Having never gotten into the trenches with us, it was as if they remained on the sidelines shouting instructions from a safe distance. Their compassion seemed to be dependent on Windsor's degree of remorse. In every instance, the comfort offered was short-lived. People were busy and they had to move on to the next "problem."

Some church leaders told me that after all I was Billy Graham's daughter and therefore I had lots of resources! In actual fact, our immediate family was the only support network

Windsor had, and we were stretched very thin. We felt ignored, "too hot to handle"—and very, very needy.

A Mother Is a Mother

Once, I tried to tell a pastor how Windsor wanted to be congratulated as a mother, one who had carried a child to term only to voluntarily give that baby to another woman. I wanted him to see how Windsor (and others like her) deserved some measure of recognition for that act of love. The pastor refused to consider my viewpoint. He said that she should not expect to be congratulated or treated as a legitimate mother because her child had been born out of wedlock and released for adoption.

To me, this didn't seem to represent Jesus' viewpoint. After all, He was born under a cloud of suspicious parentage. Certainly, He understood.

"One day that 'problem,' that 'mistake,' will wrap his little arms around you."

Do you congratulate a birthmother? Of course. She carried a baby to term and went though labor and delivery. She is a mother. A woman becomes a mother when she decides to put the needs of her child above her own needs. That's also how an adoptive mother, who has not gone through labor and delivery, becomes a legitimate mother. When she chooses to put that child's needs above her own, she becomes a mother.

You congratulate both kinds of mothers.

One of Sara's sons, who had become like a brother to Windsor, gave her a balloon with the words, "Way to Go!"—blessedly overlooking the fact that this child was "illegitimate." Windsor's child may have come out of "proper" sequence, but she is a blessing and not a mistake.

I once heard a story of a couple in the Midwest who found out their 16-year-old was pregnant out of wedlock. Heartbroken, they went to their pastor. He responded, "Isn't that wonderful!" They were nonplussed by such response. What could he mean? He responded, "One day that 'problem,' that 'mistake,' will wrap his little arms around you." He said, "All your problems should turn out that way." What a great insight by a very wise pastor!

THE NEXT CHAPTER

Windsor had released her child in late July. For the remainder of the summer, she settled down and was delightful company. She stuck pretty close to home, and we tried to do special things with her. She didn't want to go to church because it made her feel like a "scarlet woman."

I remember catching her watching "trash TV" more than once. The people on those shows had problems that made Windsor's life seem like a walk in the park!

The plan all along had been for her to go back to her public high school in August. She had kept up with her academic work so that she would be able to graduate with her class. But Windsor soon found that she did not fit in. She was no longer a teenager. Her friends were incredulous that she "gave her baby away" and they cruelly ostracized her. The "good kids" didn't want her around for fear she would be a bad influence. The youth leaders at church didn't know what to do for her either; they had no training in this area, so they did nothing. She was a "hot potato."

Naturally, Windsor gravitated toward those who didn't make her feel so bad about herself, those who had made the same or worse choices. I watched in dismay as she began spiraling downward, causing sorrow upon sorrow for herself and others. She began to date again. These young men were interested in only one thing. Windsor was desperately looking for love—someone to make her feel whole again. Things deteriorated rapidly. I told Windsor that if she didn't live by our rules she would have to move out. Unwilling to cooperate, she decided to leave.

How wrenching! I begged her to reconsider, fully aware of the danger of what she was doing. Windsor moved in with a variety of people. On one occasion, I had to ask the police to help me extricate her from a place.

Verbally abusive with me and the rest of the family, Windsor indicated to us by her behavior that she was trying to keep her pain at bay. I felt so helpless. Watching her increased my own pain to levels I didn't know I could feel. It was as if my child were drowning and I could only watch from the shore, running back and forth, screaming for help—and no one would pay attention.

This went on for almost a year.

In May, she informed me she was pregnant again. When she told me, I wept; I could not go through it again. I told her she was on her own this time.

She found a counselor who tried to help her see the destructive patterns in her life. We spent hours in his office. Eventually, he was instrumental in getting her into college. It was so important for her to have goals and to see that there was life beyond the hurt.

That summer, she spent two months back in Philadelphia with Sara. Although I had told Windsor that she was on her own, I could not abandon her, and in September we moved her into a small apartment at the college, where she did well in her studies.

In November, she gave birth to a little boy. I brought them home for the Thanksgiving weekend. As she attempted to nurse him, trying so hard to be a good mother, I felt so much pity for her. Although she desperately wanted to keep him, I felt that the odds against this going well were just too great. How would she support him and care for him?

My heart was guarded. Her son was a dear little thing, but I did not want to let him in. My own anger with Windsor was blocking this relationship. I felt she had taken advantage of my love for her and had run roughshod over my heart, not just once or twice, but over and over. I was afraid to open myself up for more hurt and pain. It wasn't the baby's fault, but we had been through so much and my emotions had gone flat.

Windsor decided not to go back to college. I felt I just could not shoulder the responsibility of helping her take care of her son. Her father, who lived in Dallas, told her she could live with him. She went down at Christmas and remained there until summer when she decided to come back to Virginia. Still unable to conform to our rules, she went to live with another family. We saw her from time to time and welcomed her and the baby whenever they came by for a visit. Slowly, my heart opened to the baby, and just like her little girl had done, he nestled into my heart and found a home. I longed to gather them both under my wing, but I knew that established boundaries were important to keep.

Eventually, she moved to Philadelphia to start her new life.

PEACE

I remember how I felt when Windsor told me that she was not going to release this baby for adoption. I got up, hugged her and told her that I was glad she was settled with it and now could move forward. When she left the room, I picked up my Bible and my eyes fell on the verse, "The earth is the LORD's, and the fulness thereof; the world, and they that dwell therein" (Ps. 24:1, *KJV*). In my heart, I felt an unexplained peace that could only have come from God.

Windsor and her baby boy belonged to God, and He loved them more than I did. He would take care of them.

WINDSOR'S STORY

Once I began to feel again, the realization began to sink in: I was a teenaged mother who had just released her baby up for adoption and I didn't fit in anywhere.

At church, I didn't feel like I belonged because they hadn't accepted me when I was pregnant, and I felt ashamed. When I attended the Christian youth groups, most of the kids didn't take any time or make an effort to get to know me. I had been labeled, and they didn't want to change their minds about me. A couple of girls did make the effort when I was still numb, but once I began to deal with my heartache they couldn't understand. I became angry, distant and eventually shut them out.

At school, a lot of my "friends" abandoned me. They ridiculed me for my decision, saying that I had given my baby away. They didn't care how much I loved my daughter. I was too damaged for the good kids. Every waking moment was filled with trying to mend myself—anything to provide me relief from this pain. Eventually, I found comfort in the "unwanted" crowd and they became a temporary Band-Aid. When I was around these kids, I didn't have to think about what I had done or how much I had disappointed my parents. I got instant gratification, and for the moment, the pain was less. My spiral downward didn't stop until I had nothing left.

During this time, my home life was falling apart. I began to feel really alone. My mother didn't talk to me about what had happened. She never told me how she hurt, what she thought or felt about the whole situation. She just made it look as though she had moved on and it was a passing thought. I was so angry that my family wanted to ignore the fact that my life had stopped for nine months and that I had a baby girl being raised by someone else. No one acknowledged that I had done a loving, strong and courageous thing. The whole episode was ignored. I felt so very alone. No longer did I even fit into the one place I was born to fit into, my family.

My relationship with my mother was a mess. We were no longer in the same book, much less on the same page. I loved her, but hated her with equal passion. I will never forget the day my mother told me to go find a grave site on our family property and bury my daughter's memory there. She felt I needed to imagine her dead in order to move on. In complete shock and anger, I told my mother she was a b—h. She slapped me and I left the house, not to return for a couple of months. My mother says I took all of my emotions out on her, and that is possibly true. I was angry at her because she didn't communicate with me and just tried to sweep everything under the rug.

CHERIE'S STORY

I really didn't fit in. Whether it was going back to school or moving back home, I felt like I could no longer relate to people as I had just nine months before. All my friends talked about were boys and what party was going on and who was dating whom. These things I used to have in common with my friends now seemed so trivial. I had matured far beyond my years. I had just given birth to another human being, something they would not be able to understand for years. Going back to their level felt like regressing.

I am not suggesting that you go out and get new friends who are "grown-ups." I am saying that once you start hanging out again, you will have to come to a happy medium that works for you. Figure out which activities you may still like and which friends you can tolerate. Some of them still have their heads in the clouds and have no clue as to how much bigger the world is outside of them. Spend your time with the people who will encourage you.

Your life will never be the same again, because you cannot erase the past nine months. But now you can take a wealth of knowledge from your experience, and you can apply it to help others (and yourself) not to make the same mistake.

SARA'S GUIDANCE

You have just been through levels of loss and grief that others aren't likely to experience—ever. Now you are going to return to high school, college or a job where you will listen to your friends talk about their boyfriends, husbands, the teachers they don't like or the boss they hate. Somehow, this all seemed so much more important last year than it does now. How can comparing nail polish colors match up to such a life-altering experience?

You will want to scream, "Do you people have any *idea* what I have just gone through?" You will find that you just won't fit in where you used to. Things that were important before aren't now. Part of you doesn't even want to fit in. Yes, you are still young, but now you have added a new title to your resumé: mother. That puts you in a category with much older women with whom you don't fit in either. Most of them have not released their children for adoption, which means they have no understanding of what you have been through. The truth is, they probably don't care.

It is important to make an effort to cultivate healthy and supportive friendships. Because of your experience, certain people may be attracted to you for all the wrong reasons and others will avoid you for those same reasons. You may need to protect yourself from some of them. Some people will understand your decision, but most won't. Don't feel the need to explain anything unless people want to hear.

You may be overcome with emotions at unexpected times. Your grief and sadness will be so deep that sometimes you will feel like you are going to cave in and die. Your need for counseling or a support group is critical now, to help you deal with the pain and loss. It has been my experience that young women who do not deal head-on with this experience are almost certain to repeat it.

You may not require long-term counseling, but you should receive it as long as you feel it is helping. The best idea is to look for a birthmother support group or begin one yourself. There you will able to talk with young women who share your experience. You will meet girls who can become your friends, and some of them will be able to show you the way not only to survive this experience but also to thrive.

Your relationship with your family has also changed, especially your relationship with your mother. You now know what she went through to give birth to you. However, giving birth is where the similarity of these experiences ends. Her response to your experience will be very different from yours. Please don't mistake her different response for not caring. Your mother has just lost her grandchild, her child's child, which is no small thing. You may feel that you were forced into releasing your child and feel anger toward your mother because of this. Undercurrents of tension and anger will sometimes explode into arguments. Even though you will feel safe venting your anger on her, try to talk about it instead.

Make a big effort to love your family at this time. They are your support network now, as most of the other people in your life have either moved on or have no idea what to do or say to help you.

Anniversaries. Every month for the first year, you will relive the experience on the date of your child's birth. This is somewhat true for all mothers, but your situation is different. Because of your decision to release your child for adoption, you are not able to celebrate in the same way other mothers do. Consequently, on the anniversary of your child's birth, you will be filled with grief and pain instead of joy and laughter. This pain will diminish over time, but it never completely goes away.

> *You will want to scream, "Do you people have any idea what I have just gone through?"*

I had a birthmother call me, crying hysterically, because it was the three-month anniversary of her daughter's birth and she hadn't remembered until late in the day. She was crying because she was afraid she was eventually going to forget her altogether. That, of course, won't happen. Your child will always be part of you no matter how much time passes.

If you and the adoptive parents have agreed that they will allow you to send your child a gift on his or her first birthday and subsequent birthdays, you will be able to celebrate in that way. If not, do something special for yourself on your child's birthday. Commemorate the value of what you have done by giving life and providing a loving, stable home for your child.

Also be aware of the impact of Mother's Day. You are going to feel as though someone has pulled your heart out, ground it up into small pieces and shoved it back into your chest. Every time you see a card or a commercial that refers to Mother's Day, you will feel as though someone is pouring salt onto your wounded heart. It will be very important to you to be recognized as a mother, but people won't know that. Please don't get angry with them for not knowing what to do. Tell them what you need.

Photographs. Depending on the frequency you have agreed upon with the adoptive parents, you will probably be getting pictures of your child. Beware! Usually you will get the first pictures within the first three months, and you will be seeing a child who does not look like the newborn you held in your arms. The pictures themselves may show your child in the arms of "that woman!" As much as this hurts, it is part of the life you have chosen for yourself and your child. You will have to learn to live with this, knowing that time heals.

You will feel as though this is not your child at all now. Even the name may be different from the one you chose. As your child grows and changes, it will begin to seem as though you are looking at a total stranger in the photos. In many ways you are. But again, you are and always will be your child's mother.

Naming your child. I strongly recommend that you give your child a name of your choosing. In the hospital, you will have the chance to fill out forms to get an original birth certificate with your name and your child's name on it. I would encourage you to do this. You can put this into a scrapbook along with your hospital name tag, greeting cards and anything else you want.

But as you know, the adopting couple may or may not choose to use the name you have chosen. Some may, and some will use part of the name, but some may not want to use any of it. As much as this will hurt, this is part of the process of healing. More often than not, when the adoptive parents write to you, they will refer to your child by the name you gave him or her, but after a while you need to tell them they can use the name they have chosen. It doesn't change your relationship with your child, but it is a step in the direction of recognizing the need to accept that your child is being raised by someone other than you. Privately, you can think of your child by the name you chose.

Reunions. I don't recommend visiting your child, especially early on. It would be like ripping a scab off a healing wound. This being said, some birthmothers feel a need to have one last good-bye with their child months down the road when the emotions are not quite so strong. If the adoptive parents agree to this and it can be done before the child is two years old, do it. But if you do, realize that you will be risking undoing all the healing that has taken place up to that point.

At the time of release, you will have been asked to sign a paper that declares whether or not you want your child to be able to contact you when the child turns 18. Just signing yes to this does *not* guarantee it will happen. It merely means you are giving the court permission to allow your child the opportunity to contact you.

One advantage in an open adoption is that you will have ongoing contact with the adoptive family, so neither you nor your child will have to hunt the other down. But because you will know where your child is, you will be tempted to want to initiate the reunion. Don't! A successful reunion can take place only when both parties want it to happen, and this should be when the child is capable of handling something this emotional in nature. Assuming you will always want the reunion to occur, be understanding and allow your child to come to you.

Also be aware of the possibility that as you mature, get married and have a family, you may not want to have this reunion. You need to allow that your feelings may change. You won't believe that now, but don't rule out the possibility.

Other triggers. For every birthmother there will be different events that will trigger memories and dredge up the pain all over again. This includes seeing babies in television shows, in commercials, in magazines and in malls. You may wonder, *Is that one the same age as my child?* It will hit you: *Someone else is pushing my child through a mall.*

If you continue to live at the address you gave the hospital, you will begin to get mail for new mothers and babies. Be prepared for this. You could ask someone to intercept the mail so that you can avoid seeing things that will trigger waves of emotion. Time and distance will help diminish the intensity of these feelings.

Recommendations

Birthmother

- Get counseling.
- Talk.
- Allow yourself to grieve.
- Admit your perspective on life has changed and learn who you are now.
- Realize that some of your friends won't understand.
- Try to find people who do understand and support you and your decision.
- Reach out and stay involved in life.
- Be aware of unexpected reminders and waves of emotion.

Support Network

- Listen.
- Acknowledge and share the grief.
- Help the birthmother focus on goals and the future.
- Praise her courage, sacrifice and love.
- Try not to be affected by others' opinions.
- Help the birthmother find counsel.

Chapter 12

The Ripple Effect

Noelle

I was a junior at Samford University. Because of my parents' divorce, college had become a refuge. My roommate had a stable family, and I enjoyed experiencing a "normal" family because of that. In addition, my academic adviser and his family welcomed me into their lives. My roommate, Chris, and I had settled into a routine and we drew close, like sisters. I felt blessed.

I love Windsor dearly. She is my only sister, and she has both looked up to me and, sometimes, competed with me and made me want to choke her. But bottom line—she's my little sister and I love her.

Soon Chris adopted Windsor too. Windsor would come to visit me at school and she seemed to enjoy my friends. We'd include her on our ski trips, and we talked by phone frequently, often with Chris joining in our conversations.

One day, Windsor called me. She said she had something to tell me. Chris could see by my expression that I was upset, so she got on the phone too. Windsor told me she was pregnant. At age 16!

> *Bottom line—she's my little sister and I love her.*

Our first response was to comfort and reassure Windsor. We wanted her to know we loved her and would be there for her—no matter what. As we hung up the phone, my mind was spinning. In some ways, I was not surprised. My sister's willfulness and inappropriate behavior with boys seemed to have made this outcome inevitable.

I went back to my studies, a true refuge now. I didn't have to think too much about what was going on at home; I didn't have to deal with it every day. But there were knots in my stomach.

Windsor's experience became part of my story too. It affected our whole family. Graham (our brother), Windsor and I had gone through the devastation of our parents' divorce and now we were dealing with this pregnancy. I felt as if we were the black sheep of the family, no longer loved quite the same because we weren't perfect.

I agreed that Windsor was not ready to raise a child and that adoption was her best option. I supported her and loved her. I had met the adopting couple and liked them very much. I thought Windsor had made a wise choice and that the baby would have a wonderful home.

That summer, I spent six weeks in Rwanda working with Samaritan's Purse, an international relief organization. I had a great experience, and I was eager to share about it and show my photographs. However, I came home to the imminent birth of Windsor's baby.

Mom wasn't home when I got there; she was in Philadelphia with Windsor. So I got in my car and drove to Philadelphia to deal with Windsor. My brother had flown in from Dallas, so we were all there. No one was particularly interested in my African experience at such a time.

Windsor gave birth to a baby girl early on July 25. We all piled into her room the next morning to be with her and see the baby she had named Victoria Windsor.

What a beautiful baby, so petite—with a head full of hair. We all fell head over heels in love. The child was no longer Windsor's but ours. I now wanted to keep her and could only imagine how torn Windsor must have been at the idea of giving Victoria over to some other woman. And Windsor did vacillate. Boy, did she ever! It created turmoil. We all had to keep reminding each other that the decision Windsor had made months before when emotions had not been so high was still the right decision.

The time arrived to release the baby. It was a very emotional time. We all cried. I was concerned for my mother and the heartache she was enduring. It is hard to see your parent distraught and you can do nothing to make it better. I was so upset that I threw myself into exercise, working out twice a day and engaging my eating disorder like a long-lost friend. Windsor was harder on herself than anyone else, expressing shame and remorse.

Back at home for the rest of the summer, I included Windsor in most of my activities and enjoyed her in a whole new way. She was compliant and thoughtful, and her joy had come back. I welcomed this Windsor with delight. For the rest of the summer, we had peace in the house. Yes, we talked about Victoria—often. Yes, we looked at the photos and the videos sent by the adoptive parents. I hoped and prayed that we were moving on and healing.

The deadline for finalization of the adoption came. At the last minute, Windsor called the adoptive couple to bring Victoria back. She had decided that she couldn't go through with the adoption. Talk about emotions! I was angry that she had waited until the last minute. I was furious at her for putting our family though this, not to mention what she was doing to the young couple. They had had Victoria for a full month. They had bonded with her! How could Windsor do this? This was one of the times I wanted to choke her.

She settled down, the adoption did happen, and we made plans to move on. I went back to Samford University, glad I wouldn't have to deal with this situation every day anymore. Windsor was looking forward to joining her senior class at the local high school.

It would prove to be a bumpy ride. As soon as she got back to school, Windsor began to run with the wrong crowd. Eventually, she left home to bounce from house to house, none of them good. I was angry for what she was putting Mom through. How could she do this to all of us? During that year she came to visit me. Chris and I tried to talk some sense into her.

In May, the family gathered in Washington to participate in my grandparents' receiving of the Congressional Medal of Honor in the Capitol Rotunda. Later that month, we all gathered for Windsor's graduation.

Before that event, Windsor had revealed she was pregnant—again. More anger. She had been given so much. It was like she had traded her inheritance for something cheap, unsatisfying. I felt she had settled for crumbs when she could have had the whole cake! I was confronted with a choice. I could abandon Windsor, or I could love her with unconditional love. I chose the latter. Our pride that she had been able to complete high school on time with her class was subdued by our knowledge that she was pregnant under her robe. But I loved her and would support her through another pregnancy.

Windsor went to summer school, anticipating entry into college. I went back to Samford. At the end of the summer, Mom got Windsor settled into a little apartment near her college and she began classes. Members of the faculty were very helpful and kind to Windsor. I was hoping she would love college and begin to form a future for herself.

The baby arrived Thanksgiving week. Mom was with her at the birth. Windsor called me to tell me she had given birth to a little boy. Mom drove them home for Thanksgiving, and we all got to meet Wyatt. After Thanksgiving, Mom took Windsor and her baby back to school to finish the semester.

Windsor had decided not to release Wyatt. I could understand her decision, but I didn't know if she would be a good mother. Could she raise this child by herself? I began to wonder if I should raise him myself. I was finishing college and maybe I would be more stable than Windsor. Mom had told her she couldn't live at home, so she decided to go live with Dad in Dallas for a short while. Eventually, Windsor moved back to Philadelphia to live.

It's working out well. My sister is a good mother, and her son is a delightful little boy. I too have a child of my own, and now I have a mother's perspective.

Windsor has had many obstacles—facing teenaged pregnancy twice and being a single mom. Yet she has trudged through and persevered, at times not graciously or easily, but she has done it.

Windsor could have chosen to have an abortion each time, but she did not. That in and of itself is a courageous decision in light of today's culture. In choosing life for her children, she gave a gift of life to the adoptive couple as well as to our family. My husband and I love Wyatt as if he were our own. As he gets older, each year he works his way deeper into our hearts. We find enormous pleasure in being his aunt and uncle. When he comes for visits, he and my husband make their breakfast trip out for doughnuts. There have been beach trips, learning to ride horses and learning to be a big cousin to our daughter. Needless to say, Wyatt is a gift, and we are thankful to Windsor for that gift.

> *In choosing life for her children, she gave a gift of life to the adoptive couple as well as to our family.*

Windsor and I have grown closer. She is a good mother to Wyatt, and I tip my hat to her for all she has been through and currently does as a single mom. God has taken the broken pieces of her life and is making something beautiful from them. I am witness to that.

CHERIE'S STORY

Your pregnancy affects your family more than you could imagine. One day a year or so after my son was born, I was upset and screaming at my mother, "You made me release my baby for adoption!" or some false statement like that, knowing full well that she would have loved to bring that baby home. (It had been entirely my decision to release him.) To my surprise, my mother (who seldom yells—ever) screamed, "Let me tell you how I hurt because you released my grandbaby!"

Oohhh! No, she didn't just say that. All of a sudden I realized how I had released her grandbaby. It was a great reality check. That whole year she had to have been hurting about that and I hadn't known it until then. The night I had him, she had stayed up, and as I slept, she went to the nursery and rocked my baby all night long.

I also found out that after our release ceremony, my sister, with whom I had been fighting for years, had turned to my mother and said, "Can't we just take him home?" Wow—I had hurt her too—she had loved her nephew and it had torn her up inside to see him go.

SARA'S GUIDANCE

When you begin this journey, you will be convinced that no one but you is scared, sad, angry or hurting. That is not true. Those in your support network are experiencing the same emotions you are, just not with the same intensity or as often. To you it will seem as though their lives have not changed, but remember, everybody deals with crises in different ways. Just as a stone is thrown into a pond and the ripples are generated from there to the shore, so it is with an unplanned pregnancy. Every one of the people who is involved in the life of the pregnant woman will be affected by her pregnancy and the decisions that follow. Some of these people won't do or say the right thing—or say or do anything at all. Give those close to you the time they need to process the information and decide how they see themselves fitting into the picture. Some won't want to fit in at all, and that choice has to be respected (not liked, but respected).

You will want everybody, especially the baby's father, to hurt as much as you do. He can't, for a lot of reasons. As a man, he's not able to have the same connection that you have with your child. He will never feel a baby move inside him and never experience the pain of bringing a baby into the world. So rather than waste a lot of energy being angry at him, try to bring him into the experience as much as you can by including him in as many of the decisions as he is willing to be a part of. Remember that this child is the grandchild of his parents as well as your parents.

Your pregnancy affects everyone in your circle of influence: your parents, the birthfather's parents, siblings on both sides, grandparents, close friends of yours and your families and coworkers of all of the above. This is the ripple effect. Do you see how one moment in time, nine months earlier, can have an everlasting effect on many people in our lives?

During one of the many release ceremonies in which I have been involved, the baby was being prayed over by the birthparents before handing her over to the adoptive parents. I watched the youngest sister of the birthmother gasp for breath as she sobbed. She understood why her sister was making the choice and she loved the adoptive family, but this was her niece, her big sister's baby, and a member of her family. She felt, *How could anyone give away a member of our family?* But that is exactly what her sister was doing, and it hurt her immensely.

Try to let all those in your support network know that you are aware of the fact that this is an experience for which there is no preparation. They need to be given permission, by you, to express their grief in whatever way they choose. Experiencing grief is good and healthy, and we must not take it from them, nor should we allow others to take it from us. This is what is called good and healing grief.

Recommendations

Birthmother

- Be aware that others hurt too.
- Don't expect the birthfather to feel the way you do.
- Accept that there will be a lot of unspoken thoughts and feelings.

Support Network

- Acknowledge how this has affected you.
- Listen to all involved.
- Don't assume you know how anyone else feels.

Chapter 13

Birthfathers

Ruth

Early in Windsor's first pregnancy, a counselor brought together the birthfather, his mother and us to talk over the birthfather's plans. It was an awkward meeting to say the least. His mother made naïve excuses for him and portrayed him as wanting to go on to a university. He was not college material by any stretch of the imagination. His actual ambitions were very low.

He himself was very up front about the fact that he did not love Windsor and did not want to marry her. He did seem to feel some responsibility—I will give him credit for that—he just was not willing to carry it too far. He was young and scared.

When he had met with us in the pastor's office earlier, the young man had told Windsor that he didn't like to be around her because she was angry with him all the time, that he was not in love with her and that he did not want to live with her. Tears had coursed down her cheeks as his words broke her heart. He had made so many promises. He had told her he loved her and she had believed him, desperately. Now her belief was all collapsing around her, and she was going to have to bear, alone, the consequences for the actions of both of them. He had humiliated her in front of everyone there. She felt so alone and betrayed.

My heart broke for my daughter. Her childhood was over. Her dreams, dashed. And he just walked away. She wanted revenge; she wanted him to pay in some way. I couldn't blame her, but I knew that there was no adequate way for her to feel satisfied. There would be no justice.

He did walk away. After the baby was born, Windsor followed him one day to his workplace to try to force him to look at his daughter's photograph. He ignored her. She created quite a scene; her fury knew no bounds.

> *He had told her he loved her and she had believed him, desperately.*

Windsor did keep in touch with his mother from time to time. When the baby was born, Windsor took pictures by to show her. His mother called the house one day, and I answered the phone. When she said she cared about Windsor, I lost it!

She who had not given Windsor so much as a quarter for a soda during this whole ordeal! I told her never to call again. I'm sorry about it now. Looking back, I realize that I had to take my frustration out on someone and she just ended up being the one that day. Perhaps her phone call was her way of trying to bridge the troubled waters, but at that moment I was not open to mere pleasantries.

SAME SONG, SECOND VERSE

Eventually Windsor found a young man who promised to fulfill her dreams of a home and family. She declared that this was the one she would marry.

His ambition was to ride bulls for a living. At the time he was hauling truckloads of hay for a local farmer. He had not finished high school. We tried to give him the benefit of the doubt, inviting him for dinner and trying to get to know him. Our inquiries about his future plans did not reassure us! We expected a repeat of the same story.

Before long, Windsor was pregnant and he was gone. He didn't want to meet with us to discuss his responsibility. He would not answer the phone and his parents were hostile. As far as he was concerned, it was over and he was out the door.

These two young men abandoned their children and my brokenhearted daughter. There were times I would have happily boiled them in oil! But God has given me the grace to forgive them. On another day, in another situation, I am sure I would have found them to be nice, polite young men. I am grateful that they did not encourage Windsor to terminate the pregnancies, secretly or overtly. They were young and scared, and they felt trapped.

In spite of them, their children are alive and well loved. Windsor can now say, "God has made me fruitful in the land of my suffering" (Gen. 41:52).

SARA'S GUIDANCE

I have often said that the men involved in any birth process suffer from the "Joseph Syndrome," because of the unfortunate emphasis that we all put on the new mother and baby, forgetting there is also a new father. In the case of an unplanned pregnancy, there is also a new father, even though, more often than not, he is nowhere to be found. Then we have the father of the birthmother, who is facing some very hard issues as well. His little girl is having a baby, and often he feels as though he didn't protect her enough.

> *If you are fortunate enough to have the baby's father actively involved, keep him involved, regardless of your personal feelings for him at this point.*

In unplanned pregnancies, it is unusual for the birthfathers to take an active role in the birth and decision-making process for the child. Most deny being the father, or if they do admit to it, they will usually tell the mother, "Do whatever you want," abdicating all responsibility. We sometimes refer to these men as sperm donors, since the title "father" implies something they are not.

If you are fortunate enough to have the baby's father actively involved, keep him involved, regardless of your personal feelings for him at this point. This is his child, and believe it or not, he has feelings too, even though they are different from yours.

Most young men tend to feel they and their opinions are not wanted or needed in pregnancy-related issues. It is true that a woman can abort her child without the permission of the father, but she cannot release the baby for adoption without his cooperation. And of course, if she decides to parent the child, the father will be financially responsible until the child is 18.

The Importance of a Dad

As a society, we tend to overlook the role of fathers in the lives of our children. Nevertheless, the single most important factor in a young woman's relationship with men in her life is her relationship with her father. Statistically:

- Children from fatherless homes are 20 times more likely to end up in jail.[1]
- 90 percent of runaway children are from fatherless homes.
- 71 percent of teenage pregnancies are to children of single parents.[2]

So all of you men reading this book need to realize, whether you are the birthfather, grandfather or just an interested young man, that you are a very important part of the life of your child. Your sons will want to be like you, and your daughters will compare every man they ever date to you. Fathers teach their children things mothers can't: how to be a man and how to love and treat a woman. Fathers can give their homes a feeling of safety; it's as if nothing bad will ever happen while Dad is home. Fathers, please don't forget how important you are.

BROWN CALDWELL'S STORY

My wife, Giselle, had sensed that something was wrong, but even though I have a close relationship with our daughter Joy, I never dreamed that she was having premarital sex—or that she was pregnant. She was attending community college, making very good grades, observing her curfew and informing us where she could be reached when she was out. She even continued to wear her promise ring, a ring worn as a pledge to remain pure. Many of her friends were involved with drugs, but Joy had convinced me that she could be around drug users without using drugs herself.

Joy told Giselle that after hearing the guest speaker on "Right to Life Sunday" at church (where I am the pastor), she had gone to the crisis pregnancy center. She had just found out that she was three months pregnant.

I was numb when Giselle told me. The words registered, but they wouldn't sink in. I wrote Joy a letter in which I assured Joy that I loved her, that her mother and I were thankful that she wasn't going to abort her baby, and yet there was no ignoring the sin of the situation, which would have to be faced. I bought a single yellow rose and placed it with the letter for Joy to find.

We told Joy that we would support her in her decisions but that we couldn't provide a home for her and her baby. The very last thing that she wanted to do was to hurt the life she was bringing into this world. She was adamant from the outset that marriage to her friend who had fathered the baby was not an option. Rather soon in the days after she found out she was pregnant, Joy decided that it would be a mistake to keep the baby. She felt that as a single mom she couldn't provide a warm home environment or financial stability. In one sense, we were sad to know that our first grandchild would be a stranger to us, but we both agreed with Joy's decision.

My biggest struggle during this time was questioning whether I had failed as a father, and my wife wondered whether she had failed as a mother. Why would Joy do this to us? Our love for her had not been destroyed, but all trust in the relationship had vaporized in a few rotations of Earth. In particular, we wondered if Joy could be trusted to stop using drugs and to avoid her old friends. Because we have three other daughters, we especially wanted to keep drugs out of our home. This was a volatile subject. Eventually, Joy chose to live primarily with a former church family whose daughter was her closest friend (and who was not involved with that group). We felt that provision of this sanctuary for her was a godsend, and we maintained frequent contact with her.

Joy's pregnancy threw my entire vocation into a time of uncertainty. Within a few days, we discovered that the scourge of drug usage among Joy's friends included other church families. Obviously, this was going to be more traumatic to the church than I had anticipated.

I called a special meeting of the governing body of the church, at which I offered a letter of resignation accompanied by a letter of explanation and apology that Joy had written voluntarily. The elders not only voted to refuse the letter of resignation but also to support Joy fully in the days ahead. They sent a letter of explanation to the members of the church along with copies of our two letters. By and large, the church handled the news well, although because of this issue (largely the drug usage more than the matter of the pregnancy) some people left the congregation in the months ahead.

Sometimes I think about what I wish I had done differently. The crisis center staff helped us with family counseling early in the process, and they were more than willing to do more.

My entire family might have gained some perspective by accepting more counseling. But we didn't. Sara Dormon bore most of the burden as well as the brunt of the backlash, such as it was.

We are still fewer than two years down the road from all of this, so hindsight is not yet as clear as it will become. One thing is clear: God is working the situation out for the good of everyone involved, as He promises to do.

Giselle and I are very proud of how Joy has rebounded. She herself has initiated some additional counseling, which has helped her to resolve some lingering issues. She is still in school, and she maintains a full-time job. She has made new friends while showing discretion in keeping many of her former friends.

We know that our grandchild, Brynne, enjoys a wonderful Christian home. But, even though Joy shares with us the pictures of her and information about her whenever she gets it, we have lost the chance to be part of our granddaughter's life, probably for all of our days, and we will always have that undercurrent of sadness.

(Joy Caldwell's story is in chapter 17.)

Recommendations (for the men)

Birthfather

- Remember, you are in this together.
- Listen to each other.
- Respect each other's feelings.
- Know your legal rights.
- Face your actions with honesty.

- Find a man you respect and get his counsel.
- Assume your responsibility.

Support Network

- Love the birthfather.
- Support his decisions.
- Listen to him.
- Don't condemn him: Forgive him.

Notes

1. "Effects of Fatherlessness (US Data)," *Center for Children's Justice.* http://www.childrensjustice.org/fatherlessness2.htm (accessed July 16, 2004).
2. "Statistics," *Center for Children's Justice.* http://www.childrensjustice.org/stats.htm (accessed July 16, 2004).

Chapter 14

Life as a Single Mom

Windsor

It is 5:15 A.M. when the alarm sounds and the madness of the day begins. I pull on some clothes, throw in a load of laundry and begin to work out for an hour. After my workout, I run upstairs to get a shower before I have to wake up my son, Wyatt, at 6:30 A.M. to begin his day. While he is getting dressed, I am making breakfast, packing his lunch and getting his stuff ready for school. We run out the door by 7:15 A.M., barely in time to catch his bus.

A smile, a kiss and the question, "Who loves you?" (answer: "Jesus") send him off for his day. His smell, simple smile and the three words "I love you" keep me going throughout my day.

> *His smell, simple smile and the three words "I love you" keep me going throughout my day.*

After he is safely on the bus, I run home to do another load of laundry, get dressed, put on my makeup, make my lunch and run out the door, all before 8:15 A.M. The drive to work allows me to get my second wind.

Life as a single mom is not easy. My days are fast, draining and unexciting. Every day I struggle to get out of bed to go to a job that will pay the bills.

I would love to be a stay-at-home mom, to fully participate in my child's school functions and to greet him when he gets off the bus. I am very fortunate to have Sara Dormon, who helps me with my son on a daily basis. She takes him to the bus stop on the mornings I have to go to work early, and she is there every day to greet him as he arrives home. She is there when the school calls to say he is sick or when there is a snow day. Although I am grateful, I am still jealous that she gets to spend more time with him than I do. I have such a small amount of time with my beautiful seven-year-old.

The Dormon family has adopted me. They have had their share of hard times with me, but we have always worked them out. One moment, Sara and I will be screaming at each other and the next moment, we'll be laughing. In their family I have found somewhere I fit. My son is their grandson and I am their daughter. What an honor! I can always count on them, whether it is to cry or to have someone watch my son so I can go out. Currently, I live six blocks away from them and see them on a daily basis; I even talk with them on the phone a couple of times a day. Life would be dull without their added spark.

DAILY EVENTS

When I am home from work, my time is consumed with paying bills, maintaining our house, taking care of Wyatt, keeping in touch with friends and dating. After paying the bills, I sometimes find myself crying to sleep because there is a constant struggle between paying the bills and having extras. Some days there is more than enough money, and other days there just isn't enough. I have had to learn to prioritize which bills get paid now and which get paid later. When I have extra money, of course then something in the house breaks and has to be fixed immediately.

I am very blessed to be able to afford a house that I can call my own. It has been a stabilizer in our lives. Wyatt and I both know we have someplace safe we can call home. At the same time, this safe haven demands money, time and constant maintenance. Wyatt and I will start to do projects together, but by the end I am the only one left doing the project. If something needs to be fixed, I always try to fix it on my own.

I will never forget last year when a big snowdrift somehow forced my garage door off track. When I needed something from the garage, I discovered that the door wouldn't open. After I hit the door several times, it opened, but then it wouldn't shut. My kind neighbor helped me figure out the problem and together we fixed it, and now it works fine. I was proud that, with help, I had fixed it. Another time, I had a beautiful picture that I wanted to hang in my hallway. It must have weighed 60 pounds. This petite woman hung it all by herself! I even made sure it was centered on the wall, just like a pro! The simple things frustrate me to no end, but when I can figure them out I think, *Wow, I did that by myself!*

RELATIONSHIPS

My friends are limited in number but not in quality. Sometimes I wish I had more friends, but then I realize I wouldn't have enough time to develop the close friendships I am used to. My friends are very diversified; each of them has his or her own story and has managed to weather the difficult storms of life. Many of them live in other states and I see them only maybe once a year. Most are married, but they never make me feel left out. Most of my friends are very spiritual people with an edgy side to them. They all add to my life and I am grateful that I have so much with so few. They are precious to me.

One of my best friends, Meghan, lives in Florida. I make a point to see her and her wonderful family once a year. Meghan was my roommate at the unwed mothers' home where I lived for a time before my daughter was born. I call Meghan my angel because she was my only friend when we both felt we were walking through hell. We held each other's hands when the heat was the worst. Over the years, our friendship has only become deeper. We have the kind of relationship that we can pick up right where we left off, even if we have not talked for months on end. She is the one friend who cried when I learned that my sister had given birth to a little girl, because she could appreciate how deeply painful that was for me. Meghan and I believe that because we went through some of the worst trials of our lives together, a rare bond that nothing can break has developed between us. Most people look all their lives for a friendship like ours. I am fortunate that God has blessed me with her.

The dating scene can be maddening. Most Friday nights, I am content to just be at home in my pajamas, watching a movie. But there are other times I want to get out. It is time-consuming and tiring to find good ways to meet the kind of guys I'm looking for. Some of the guys don't want a woman with "baggage." I inform such guys that my supposed "baggage" may be more obvious, but that they have some too—it's just hidden.

In Wyatt's short life I have introduced him to many of my dates. Unfortunately, he got attached to a few men, only to be let down when he found out that this wasn't going to lead to a new dad. Finally, I wised up and decided to change my approach. Now I will go out on date, and if the fellow is lucky, he will get a second date. But he has to come over after Wyatt's bedtime, and he isn't allowed to meet my son unless we have been dating six months or more. Needless to say, my son has not met one of my dates in a long time.

I can't count how many times I have had my heart broken and how much disappointment I have had to overcome in this strange area called "love." Recently, I said I would never fall in love again, and so far I still I feel that way; but in due time I will love somebody else, even if I get disappointed again. Obviously, I haven't found the right man; I even wonder if he is out there. I long for a man to come along and I will just know—and the rest of our lives will be written in that moment.

MOTHERHOOD IN ACTION

With all of this, the best and most exciting part of my life is Wyatt. Even though raising him is my biggest challenge, it is also a lot of fun.

He has been taught to focus on what he does have and not on what he doesn't have. Probably I am more sensitive than he is about his lack of a dad. I attended parents' night at his school at the beginning of this year. His teacher went over the events that would happen in the classroom in the coming year—ice-cream social, a dad's appreciation day . . . The teacher noticed my tearful look of disgust, and he pulled me aside afterward to find out what was bothering me. I told him that I am a single parent, both father and mother for my son. If I were to come in on a dad's appreciation day, it would be like broadcasting Wyatt's lack of a father. There's no good solution. For such events, my son has had many "stand-ins." Sara's entire family and mine have tried to fill the father gap.

My son notices that he doesn't have a father, and he has asked where his father is and what happened. I find these to be the hardest questions to answer. I always tell him, "Mommy and your father decided before you were born that we couldn't be together and our decision had nothing to do with you." Once I heard him tell someone his interpretation: "My dad doesn't love me or my mommy." That broke my heart, because I have tried to make sure that he wouldn't feel that way. Of course, I realize that Wyatt would think that if his father didn't want to make it work with his mommy and didn't love his mommy, then, by extension, he didn't love Wyatt either. I am grateful that he doesn't know his father. His father is still stuck in the same self-defeating patterns and is not the kind of person I would want Wyatt to emulate. Yet I will never say anything bad about his father. I don't hate his father. The choice was made and I am better for it. If by some chance my son wants to meet his father someday, I will be supportive. I will drive him to the place to meet him. I will knock on the front door with him. But I will not sit and listen to his father talk with him. My son will have to learn firsthand what I have known all along about his father. I will be right beside him to wipe away the tears.

That's one of the tough issues in our lives. There are many ups and downs, but mostly it is fairly pleasant. God knew that I needed a child who was the complete opposite of me, so He gave me Wyatt. My son is the best child I know. Of course, I am biased, but other people say it too. He is mellow, tenderhearted, kind, polite, gentle, loving, obedient and smart. Wyatt doesn't need to have my full attention or need to be entertained. This has made being a single mom easier. It is also a downfall because he doesn't demand too much and sometimes I fear I give him too little. There are hard times when he wants to talk and all I want is quiet. There are days when I scream like a mad woman because I am running late, and as a result I hurt his feelings. I do worry that my mistakes will affect him for the rest of his life. I pray daily that God will overrule my mistakes.

I try to be the best mother I can be. Every day I have to put what I want on the back burner to accommodate Wyatt's needs. There have been times when I have nothing left inside and yet he requires something more of me, I try to muster up the strength to give a little of myself to him. All it takes is a few minutes to put a smile on his face. And when I am crying, Wyatt runs straight for me, gives me a huge hug and tells me he loves me.

I like to call Wyatt a teacher because he has taught me more about life than I think I have taught him. Because I am young, we have had to grow up together, and he has had to endure my mistakes, but we have managed to recover from each one and grow stronger. There are more good moments than bad. I love it at the end of the day when he prays. He will pray for all the animals, me, his grandparents and anyone he knows who is hurting. A simple tickle fight on my bed can keep us laughing for hours. That little dance that we shared in the kitchen leaves a lasting smile. When we watch a movie together, he picks one out and we lie on the couch and cuddle. Exhausted, I am usually asleep by the end of the movie.

He teaches me simplicity. I know when he gives me a certain look and starts to smile that he will say the most amazing things. I am in awe that God gave this special little man to me. Wyatt will always try something adventurous. Last year we started taking long bike rides together. His sense of adventure has him riding well ahead of me, exploring around the next corner. He also likes going on the upside-down roller coasters with me. These simple moments are what keep me getting out of bed each day. I am honored that God has trusted me enough to allow me to handle this precious life. It isn't easy, but it is worthwhile.

A Different Kind of Motherhood

I am Wyatt's mom, but I am also the birthmother of a precious little girl who is nine. She plays soccer, swims, sings and dances in ballet recitals. When I see an envelope with her return address, my heart jumps and I can't open it fast enough. I read the letters her

> *I am the one who loved her from the beginning, carried her under my heart for nine months and still hold her in my heart every day.*

mother writes and tears stream down my face. I proudly show her pictures to anyone who will look. A lot of people don't understand why I would show her pictures around, but I say, "Why not?" I may not be the mother who tends to her needs, but I am still her mother. I am the one who loved her from the beginning, carried her under my heart for nine months and still hold her in my heart every day. These pictures confirm in my heart and mind that I made the right decision. Her life is what I dreamed for her; she has a dad who is very involved in her life, a mom who is there when she gets off the bus and a little brother to share the growing-up years. My heart aches when I see the pictures and read about her life, because I am not able to give such things to her, but it also reassures me she is right where she is supposed to be.

Forever I will live with the pain of the day I released her, and forever I will carry my daughter's newborn picture in my wallet. Please don't get me wrong and think that every day I wake up sobbing, rocking myself back and forth. The pain doesn't keep me from happiness or hinder my daily life. It is just a part of my life. I keep it inside, very secret. I don't think you ever recover from the loss of a child; you just learn to deal with it.

A couple of months ago, my mother had a speaking engagement and I went to hear her. We knew ahead of time that it would be difficult for her to speak with me in the audience, and I knew it would be hard to hear her. My mom started her speech and talked about my siblings—then she got to me. She started to go into the details of my story, with my permission. I tried to wipe away the tears so that she wouldn't see them. She talked about the courage of birthmothers, about how they do something so unselfish and heroic. When she got to the part about my letting my daughter go, we both started to cry. I was trying to stifle it, but I had to let out a squeak. When she was finished with her speech, with tears on both our faces, she introduced me as *her* brave birthmother. Even though I have learned to deal with the pain, the intensity of it can resurface with just a thought. I can't read this book without its coming back to me as if it were just yesterday.

When my older sister, Noelle, told me she was pregnant, I was happy she was having a baby, but as the time got closer, I started to dread the birth. What if it was a girl? What would I do? My daughter would be replaced. Everyone would forget but me.

On a beautiful fall day my sister delivered a baby girl. That night I cried myself to sleep. I called my good friend Meghan and we wept together. (This all sounds so selfish, but it might happen to you too, so I want to share it.) I didn't want a replacement baby. I wanted everyone to mourn the loss of my daughter forever. I postponed going to meet my niece as long as I could. Finally, I went, with dread. When I saw her I didn't want to pick her up. I was afraid I would love her. Of course I did pick her up and of course I loved her immediately. I left angry because God had taken away my daughter but was allowing my sister, who has done the right thing all along, to raise her daughter in front of my eyes. How much pain and jealousy I carried!

A couple of weeks later, I realized God wasn't being cruel to allow this. He was blessing me by allowing me to watch and participate in my niece's life. It was His way of giving me something back after my loss.

Today, I am the proud aunt of a precious little girl. I recognize that no one can replace my daughter in our hearts, because my niece has caused my family, especially my sister, to realize how very precious my daughter is and how amazing my sacrifice was.

I am careful with whom I choose to tell my story. Most of the world doesn't understand going against your natural instinct and releasing your child to another. People say really hurtful things out of their ignorance. It used to really get me down. After all, I am already hard enough on myself. Then I learned that the One who counts has forgiven me, totally and unconditionally, and that all I had to do was forgive myself. Now my self-image no longer takes a beating with people who are ignorant. I have learned to embrace those people and try to help them understand why a woman might want to release her child. I decided to become the change I wish to see in the world.

On Mother's Day three years ago, my daughter's mother told me that my daughter had asked about me and wondered if she could meet me. Those words confirmed the hope that I had carried with me through the darkest days, the hope that she would want to find me one day. I know I will see for myself those big blue eyes again, and I hope that my daughter finds a friend in me. Until then I will carry her picture, find satisfaction in watching her grow up in pictures and love her consistently—with a heart that has a piece missing.

JOY

As you have read in this book, my relationship with my family was very tattered and torn. It continued to be for a long time. I hated my mother for some of the things she did and said concerning events surrounding my pregnancies. After I released my daughter, the other members of my family seemed to just move on as if it was nothing. When Wyatt was born, at first my family reserved their love for him, and because of this, I had a lot of anger toward them. I did everything I could to eat them up, chew them to bits and spit them out. I told them horrible things. I did horrible things. But with time we have healed—slowly.

Once my family realized I wasn't going to place Wyatt for adoption as I did with my daughter, they started to participate in his life a little more. More and more my son started to form a bond with my family that has become amazingly strong. Two years ago, my mom started the tradition of taking Wyatt for two weeks during the summer. They have a great time.

Even though my family and my son were bonding, I kept myself removed from them. I had put up a wall and was just too angry with them to be a part of them. I am a family woman and

I felt, in spite of the wall, that nothing would keep me from helping them if they needed me. But I felt too wounded to fit in.

Right after my niece was born, I went on a weeklong vacation. I did a lot of thinking that week and I let go of a lot of the old issues. I had to let go of something if I was ever going to restore my relationship with my family. Without realizing it, I came home from vacation a new woman. My relationship with my family has healed. I finally feel like I fit in, in my own way. My mom and I talk on the phone every day while I'm driving home from work. If I don't call her, she calls me. My sister and I have delightful conversations about life struggles and kids. My mom and sister even ask for my advice! I have started to visit home more than I used to. We have planned two vacations this year all together, and that is the start of a new tradition. For the first time, without my mentioning my desire to move closer to home, they said they would love for me to be closer and are keeping an eye out for the right house. After all this time, we are growing closer. I even cry when I have to leave.

Is my life easy? No. Not by a long shot—never has been and never will be. But my life is *great*. As I continue to heal, I realize how much strength I have developed because of my experiences. I have two beautiful, healthy kids, a house, two families where I belong, friends and a relationship with a wonderful, forgiving God. I wish more people had the life I lead.

Chapter 15

How Should the Church Respond?

Tim Troyer

What do they want to talk about? I had wondered all evening as I waited for our guests to arrive. Earlier that day, I had received an unusual phone call from one of our church elders asking if he could bring his family to our house to talk with my wife and me. "Of course," I replied. Something in his voice had kept me from asking why.

I was a bit nervous as I opened the door, but not as nervous as my guests were. As Ben, Bonnie and their four children sat down in our living room, I could see that some of them had been crying. After a few seconds of intense silence, Ben dropped the bombshell, "Pastor Tim, Melonie is pregnant. She is going to have a baby."

A barrage of thoughts raced through my mind: *What shall I say? How can I give hope to 19-year-old Melonie? At the same time, how can I make sure that sin is dealt with properly? How should I provide comfort to the hurting family? How should I deal with my own newly triggered flood of emotions? What will happen to the baby? How will the church react to the news? Lord, please help me!*

> *It is too easy for people's problems to eclipse the fact that these are* people *in need of God's help and mercy.*

In the course of my ministry, I have forgotten many of the events and crises I have encountered, but I will never forget that evening. My wife and I assured them that we would stand with them and help them as a family through this tough time. We realized that we needed God's grace to handle this situation His way. I don't assume naïvely that I handled the crisis perfectly, but walking this young girl and her family through repentance, forgiveness and restoration taught me lessons about God, myself and those in need. Here are a few of those lessons.

Focus on people, not on problems. It is too easy for people's problems to eclipse the fact that these are *people* in need of God's help and mercy. Pastors tend to try to manage the problems and do damage control instead of identifying with the people. Frankly, that is how I felt at first in this situation. Part of me just wanted the problem to go away. I was tempted to make decisions and manage the information based on what I thought would keep the fallout to a minimum, protecting the reputation of myself, our church and others.

That was the wrong attitude! Jesus, a friend of sinners, doesn't just want our problems to go away. He (who was willing to become of no reputation for us) will never forsake us, even when we bring shame to Him.

When we refuse to identify with people who are troubled and fail to restore them to fellowship through love and humility, we are declaring that image is more important than anything else. As Christians cluck their tongues and shake their heads over the sin of abortion, they can unknowingly create an emotional environment in which a young pregnant girl would rather commit that sin than face being mistreated, ostracized and humiliated by fellow Christians. In my office, girls have wept as they described how Christian parents or relatives were pressuring them to have an abortion because they wanted to protect their reputations above all else.

We claim to know the Scriptures, but we fail to understand the heart of God. We condemn the sin without conveying God's cleansing forgiveness to the woman caught in the act. And applying the double standard that has been used for centuries, we subject only the woman (not the man) to public shame, using the Word to bludgeon the very people it was meant to protect, rescue and heal.

Although my wife and I made a deliberate decision to stand with Melonie and her family privately and publicly, the young man who was the father of the baby would not. His father was on the pastoral staff of another church in our area, and he and his family chose to distance themselves from the "problem," which made it very tough.

Deal openly but tactfully. I do not believe in airing people's dirty laundry in public. However, when sin is known publicly, dealing with it in an open and tactful way can be powerful and redemptive. Melonie knew that it was impossible to hide her pregnancy, because in a short while nature would make this obvious to everyone who saw her. I counseled her and her family to deal with it just as openly. I suggested that Melonie immediately communicate with the rest of her family and tell them what had happened, confessing her sin to the people who were most important to her and letting them know about her repentance. I encouraged her not to say, "I made a mistake," or "This was an accident," but to say, "I sinned when I made the wrong choice."

Melonie bravely did that. She asked for forgiveness and prayer, and it was tremendously healing. It enabled friends and family members to talk with her openly about her pregnancy and the struggles she was facing. The Bible tells us that he who conceals his sin will be ashamed, but he who confesses his sin and renounces it will in the end be honored (see Prov. 28:13).

After Melonie had the opportunity to tell her relatives and close friends, we had a meeting with the church leadership team. She talked with our pastors, elders and their wives. It was a sacred meeting. She also met with our former pastor, who had retired, and his wife and talked and prayed with them. Our elders and their wives told Melonie that they forgave her and would pray for her and her child. Most of our leadership team found out about her sin and her repentance at the same time, which was very helpful.

After this, I advised Melonie and her family to talk openly with our congregation. That was scary for everyone. I didn't insist that this happen but left the decision in Melonie's hands. After praying and talking with her family about it, she felt that she should say something publicly. Our pastoral staff prayed about her decision and decided that the best time would be on a Sunday morning during our regular service. We encouraged Melonie to invite all of the family members and friends with whom she had shared the information, and the church was packed. In addition, it happened that we had an unusually large number of visitors present, which made me nervous. I prayed, *Oh, God, please help us today. I don't want us just to seem like a loving and forgiving church. I want us to be one! Help!*

Partway through the service, I asked Melonie to share. The pastoral staff and her family stood with her on the platform as she read a brief statement to the congregation. Her words were well chosen and to the point. She asked the people to forgive her and to pray for her.

Then I stepped to the podium beside her and emphasized the rewards and blessings of forgiveness and God's mercy. I talked about being a redemptive community and creating a safe environment in which to confess our sins to each other and to pray for one another. I concluded by saying that the Lord had forgiven Melonie, her family and friends had forgiven her, and we as pastors and elders had forgiven her too. All that was left now was for the congregation to forgive her. Acknowledging the visitors, I addressed them as well. "You are representatives of the larger Body of Christ. Will you also forgive Melonie?" I asked for all who sincerely wanted to respond to her request for forgiveness to stand as they felt led. People began standing, many of them crying. Then, spontaneously, they began pouring to the front of the sanctuary to hug Melonie and her family. It was one of the most powerful worship services in which I have ever participated.

The outpouring of love and support was amazing. Visitors from out of town shook my hand at the door and told me that they had never been in a service like that before. Melonie got cards and letters from all over the United States from people who heard about what had happened. The most important result of all was that Melonie felt forgiven and that she could smile and hold up her head in our church. She would be facing some tough consequences ahead, but one of those would not be shame or disassociation from our church family.

> *Each human being conceived is deeply loved by God the Father and has a special intended place in His kingdom.*

There are no illegitimate children. There are only illegitimate actions. Each human being conceived is deeply loved by God the Father and has a special intended place in His kingdom. God chose for His Son to enter the world through a young, unmarried girl, and He bore the stigma of illegitimacy with dignity.

Melonie and her parents wrestled with the options of giving the baby up for adoption or keeping the child. Eventually, with the support of her family, Melonie decided to keep the baby; they felt this was God's will for them. Because they had made this decision before she spoke with our congregation, I was able to tell them that I was looking forward to the day when we would be dedicating her child in our church before the Lord.

Melonie went into labor on a Wednesday evening. I had to laugh at the timing of it. Most of our people were in small-group Bible studies all over the community. The news spread, and everyone was praying for her. After my Bible study, I went to the hospital to find that she'd had a beautiful, healthy baby girl.

More people visited Melonie and her baby in the hospital than had visited any other child ever born in our congregation!

Several months later, we dedicated Melonie's baby to the Lord on a Sunday morning, again speaking tactfully and openly about the whole situation. On Mother's Day, we gave Melonie a flower along with all of the other mothers to recognize her as a mother. We did not single her out; we just told her privately to stand with all the other mothers when they stood to be honored. My wife and I made it a point to talk with her that morning and to tell her how proud we were of her, and that we thought she was being a good mom. I told her that I was committed to pastoring her daughter and that we would always be there when she needed us and would help in any way we could.

Melonie struggled. She went through hard times and bore some tough consequences. She did experience some painful treatment in the community, some hurtful gossip. Thankfully, it wasn't from the hands of any people in her church. But her hardships drew her closer to the Lord. She began to seek God when she woke up at night to feed her hungry baby, and she became serious about her walk with the Lord, making a commitment to purity and to seeking His will for her life. She became an inspiration and encouragement to younger people in our congregation.

What has happened to Melonie since? She met and fell in love with a fine Christian young man, and they got married. I had the great pleasure of conducting the wedding ceremony. Melonie's husband adopted her daughter, and she has grown up calling him "Dad." I have the wonderful privilege of being their pastor. Melonie's daughter is a very special girl who is loved dearly by her family, grandparents, church members and classmates. I hope to see her walking down the aisle of our church, dressed in white, at her own wedding. I want to conduct that service too, and witness God's faithfulness to a new generation.

Chapter 16

Summary on Adoption Law

Debra Fox, Esq.

Because the laws of adoption vary from state to state, no uniform adoption law applies to the entire nation, although common threads link the laws of every state. What follows is an explanation of basic adoption laws, without details about any particular state's law. This is meant to be an introduction to people involved in the process of adoption. However, for guidance as to the laws of a particular state, please contact an experienced adoption attorney in that state.

AGENCY VERSUS PRIVATE ADOPTION

There are two types of adoptions available in most states: agency adoptions and private (independent) adoptions.

In an agency adoption, the birthmother contacts a licensed adoption agency to assist her in finding a family to place her baby for adoption. The advantage of agency adoption is that adoption agencies are licensed by the state and are therefore monitored on an annual basis for compliance with appropriate laws. Most states prohibit licensed adoption agencies from hiring employees who have been convicted of a crime or accused of child abuse. To help birthmothers to thoroughly consider all options besides adoption, such as foster care, parenting or having a family member parent the child, agencies are allowed to provide counseling services to birthparents and adoptive families.

In a private or independent adoption, no agency is involved. Instead, a private adoption attorney handles the case. One disadvantage of private adoption in some states is that the birthmother may not be able to get counseling. If her state does not allow adoptive families to reimburse her for counseling expenses (and, because it is a private adoption, no agency will be providing that service), the birthmother may not be able to afford counseling and may not receive it. Even so, some birthparents prefer working with an attorney for personal reasons.

In a private adoption, it is always important to know whom the attorney represents. In most states it is illegal for the same attorney to represent both the birthparents and the adoptive family, due to the inherent conflict of interest. Usually, the adoptive family hires an attorney and the birthparents have a separate attorney. In certain states, it is legal for the adoptive parents to reimburse the birthparents for legal expenses. However, some birthparents choose not to hire their own attorney at all, if their state allows them to forego legal representation.

FACILITATORS

Facilitators operate apart from licensed adoption agencies and attorneys. Adoptive parents hire facilitators, whose services are often advertised in the Yellow Pages, to locate a birthmother who will place her child for adoption with them. However, in most states, facilitators cannot do more than match a birthmother with an adoptive family. If they do, they will appear to be operating as an adoption agency without a license. Facilitators are not licensed. Because they are not licensed, there is no supervision or quality control by the state.

LEGAL DOCUMENTS

Whether birthparents decide to work with an agency or private attorney, legal papers need to be signed. Most (if not all) states require a birthmother to wait until after she delivers her baby to sign a consent or surrender of her baby for adoption. This is a protection for the birthmother. It is one thing to consider adoption while pregnant, and it is another to follow through with that decision once the baby is in the world. The thinking is that after a woman delivers a baby, she goes through emotional and physical changes that could interfere with her ability to make a good, clear, life decision. Waiting periods vary from 24 hours to 10 days. Some states have no waiting period after the baby is born, and they allow the birthmother to sign a consent immediately.

Consent-signing requirements can differ between birthmothers and birthfathers. While nearly every state requires that birthmothers wait until after they deliver before they can sign a consent, many states now allow birthfathers to sign any time before the delivery. The rationale behind this is that sometimes birthfathers are available to sign a consent earlier in the pregnancy, whereas they may not easily be found after the birth of the baby. If a birthfather is willing to consent to an adoption, most states feel it is important to give him that opportunity even before the birth of the baby. After all, birthfathers do not go through the same physical changes that birthmothers do after birth.

REVOCATION OF CONSENT

After the consent is signed, some states allow the birthparents to revoke it, or to change their minds about the adoption. In other words, if a birthparent decides he or she made the wrong decision in placing the baby for adoption, there is sometimes a window of opportunity to regain custody of the child.

The laws vary widely on this subject. For example, in some states, a consent signed by a birthmother at 72 hours after the birth of her baby is considered irrevocable. In other words, the birthparents' rights are forever terminated. In other states, the signing of a consent is viewed as an indication of the birthparents' intent, but their parental rights may not be terminated until a hearing takes place months down the road. In the intervening time between the signing of the consent and the termination hearing, the birthparents would have the right to change their minds.

In every adoption there comes a point when birthparents can no longer change their minds. Whether it is upon the signing of the consent, when a judge signs an order terminating the parental rights of the birthparent after a hearing or when the judge signs the final adoption decree, states feel that there should be some finality and security for the child, making it impossible for a birthparent to defeat an adoption.

MINOR BIRTHPARENTS

If a birthparent is considered a minor, some states have extra requirements about who must be notified. (The definition of a minor varies from state to state as well. It can be anywhere from 16 to 21 years of age, with the most common definition of a minor being somebody who is younger than 18 years of age.) Many states require that if a birthparent is a minor, the birthparents' parents must be notified of a hearing that would terminate the parental rights of their minor child. Some states go one step further than sending a mere notice to the birthparents' parents: They require that the parents of a minor also consent to the adoption. More progressive states, however, no longer require the consent of a minor's parents.

A birthparent should notify his or her parents as soon as possible about his or her intention to place a baby for adoption, since the court will usually require this anyway. If a minor's parents disagree with their child's wish to place the baby for adoption, many courts will weigh the maturity and competency of the minor birthparent against the minor's parents' reasons for not allowing the adoption. One scenario in which a court might go against the wishes of a minor birthparent to place a child for adoption is if the minor parent's parent already is raising a sibling of the baby. Many courts do not wish to separate siblings if it can be helped.

BIRTHFATHERS

Many birthmothers wonder whether they have to inform a birthfather about their pregnancy and their desire to place a baby for adoption. Regardless of what state a birthmother lives in, she is required to identify the birthfather if she knows who he is. This is because birthfathers, by virtue of being biologically connected to the child, have rights to the baby, just as the birthmother does.

Even if the birthfather knew the birthmother for only one day and he never supported her during the pregnancy or inquired about her welfare, he still has the right to know that he is the father of a baby and to oppose an adoption if he desires. Even birthfathers who are serving time in prison have rights to their children. Do not assume that a birthfather's rights will automatically be terminated just because he has had little contact with a birthmother or because he is not living a model life.

Many times a birthmother will state that she knows the first and last name of a birthfather but not his current whereabouts. In those instances, a diligent attempt must be made to find the birthfather and notify him of the adoption. Many states have paternity registries which provide a birthfather with an opportunity to notify the state that he wishes to claim paternity to a child he knows will be born or has been born. In some states, if a birthfather fails to register, he cannot be heard to assert any rights to a baby.

Even if a birthfather does not sign a consent, in most states, his parental rights can still be terminated. So long as he is not opposed to the adoption, he is not required to sign any documents in order for the adoption to move forward. Many birthfathers do not realize that allowing their child to be placed for adoption relieves them of any child support obligations forever. That is because an adoption severs all rights a biological father has to his child. He is considered a legal stranger to his child once his parental rights have been terminated. By the same token, he would not have the right to visit with the child, unless of course the adoptive family entered into an open adoption agreement with him.

When a birthmother is married to a man who is not the biological father of the baby, he is often considered the legal father of the baby. Many states presume that if a baby is conceived while the birthmother is married, her husband must be the father. Therefore, those states that make that presumption require that the husband consent to the adoption. If he chooses not to consent, then his rights need to be terminated against his will, or on an involuntary basis. Some birthmothers do not want their husbands to know about the adoption, perhaps because they have been separated from them for years and do not wish for them to know their personal business. Unless such a birthmother can produce a divorce decree, long separation does not relieve the need to notify the legal father of the adoption. If the biological mother and father are willing to submit to DNA testing, proving they are in fact the baby's parents and thereby ruling out the legal father as the actual father, it might not be necessary to notify the legal father. Whether or not this can be done depends on the willingness of the judge in the state before whom a birthparent will appear.

REIMBURSEMENT OF BIRTHPARENT EXPENSES

Also varying from state to state is the issue of whether adoptive parents can reimburse a birthparent for living expenses related to the pregnancy, birth and delivery of the baby.

Some states have very strict laws disallowing reimbursement of any expenses except for medical expenses of the baby or birthmother during the pregnancy and delivery. Other states allow the adoptive family to reimburse a birthmother for such expenses as housing, food, maternity clothes, counseling and transportation. Those states that allow adoptive parents to reimburse birthparents for these expenses usually require judicial approval. On the one hand it is argued that reimbursement of these expenses can look like bribery or coercion. ("If you let me adopt your baby, I'll give you money to make your life easier.") On the other hand, many birthmothers face extreme financial hardship in deciding to continue an unwanted pregnancy. Some birthmothers cannot continue working and may have no way of obtaining clean, safe housing during the pregnancy if not for the help of an adoptive family.

OPEN ADOPTION

In most states, it is possible for an adoption to be open. What this means is that there is some level of contact between the birth family and the adoptive family. This contact can be anything from having an intermediary send letters and pictures back and forth, while maintaining anonymity between the parties, to visiting one another periodically in one another's homes, knowing one another's names and addresses. Usually, in order for identifying information to be revealed about a birthparent or adoptive parent, the party whose information will be revealed has to consent to the release of the information. One of the most common types of open adoption is one in which the adoptive family agrees to send letters and pictures through their agency or attorney to the birthparents several times per year.

Most states do not have provisions in their laws for what happens if an adoptive family fails to live up to their agreement to maintain some sort of open relationship with the birthparents. A dissatisfied birthparent could bring some kind of legal action against the adoptive family, but there is no guarantee that he or she would prevail. Most states look at adoption as the severing of one set of relationships (the birthparents to the child) and the establishment of another set of relationships (the adoptive parents to the child). However, in at least one state, there is a provision in the law for the birthparents to have recourse if an adoptive family fails to live up to their end of the bargain. However, the law states that even if there is a legal dispute on the issue of openness, it cannot interfere with the finality of the adoption itself.

CONCLUSION

When each state draws up its adoption laws, it seeks to balance the rights of all of the parties to the adoption. The parties to the adoption consist of the birthmother, the birthfather, the adoptive parents, the child and the grandparents of the child. Many times, the wishes of all of these parties do not coincide. When that happens, it is up to a judge to decide. The guiding principle is usually whatever is in the best interests of the child. Some states give more weight to the rights of birthparents, such as when there is a longer period of revocation (or when birthparents can change their minds about the adoption). Other states attempt to give finality to an adoption sooner, terminating the birthparents' rights early on in the adoption process.

States also vary in how easy or difficult they make it for a birthfather to assert his parental rights if he objects to an adoption. Grandparents also have varying degrees of rights, depending on what state is involved.

Because this overview cannot make specific reference to the laws of each state, it is important to consult with an adoption attorney in your own state.

Chapter 17

Adoptive Parents: Firsthand Experience

Kevin Gallagher

In the past six years, my wife, Heather, and I have successfully adopted three children. The babies came from as far away as Chicago and as close as 10 miles from our home in Pennsylvania.

Now at least once a month people call us to ask if we would tell them about adoption. There are so many people who want to be adoptive parents, but they don't know where to start looking for advice. We are glad to share what we have learned through our firsthand experience, because we don't want anyone to miss out on adopting a child.

Most prospective parents have a lot of misinformation about the process of adoption. Some folks think that waiting lists go on for years. Others expect a child to cost hundreds of thousands of dollars. Still others believe that the only way to find a child to adopt is to go to China, Korea, Russia or some other far-off land. Most would-be adoptive couples are overwhelmed by the enormity of the task, not to mention the risks involved. They get scared as they think about all the what-ifs and too quickly give up their dream of having a family.

I used to believe some of the adoption myths myself. Seven years ago, Heather and I were in the ranks of the uninitiated. For years, as we hoped to become pregnant, we didn't really want to know much about adoption. I can remember brushing off the idea by thinking, *It costs too much money. Besides, where would we ever find a baby?*

> *Will we really be able to love a child that is not biologically ours?*

It was only after determining that we probably weren't going to be able to conceive that we seriously considered adoption. After being hung up for a while on whether we could give up on being biological parents without exploring even more medical techniques, we decided to move forward toward our dream of having a family by giving up our dream of having a son or daughter who looked, sounded and acted like us.

Of course, we were also plagued by the other classic fears of adoptive parents: Will we really be able to love a child that is not biologically ours? What if the birthparents change their minds and try to reclaim the child? What if the child wants to meet his or her birthparents? What if we end up having both adopted and biological children?

Those concerns seemed never-ending and they nearly overtook us. Ultimately, we just decided to take a leap of faith. We are overjoyed that we did! Family life is everything that we always dreamed it would be.

TRYING TO MAKE A BABY

Our story is typical. We married young and decided to put off having children as we pursued our careers. When we started trying to have children in our mid-20s, we found that it was not quite as easy as we had expected.

Infertility is indescribably difficult. We spent four years doing tests and procedures, but everything came down to what we called "the monthly disappointment." The process was dehumanizing, with nightly shots of fertility medication and numerous doctor appointments.

We never imagined that we would become regulars at the fertility clinic. The doctors, nurses and technicians all knew us on a first-name basis. We became almost like family, except this was a family we really didn't want to be a part of. In the midst of our frustration, we tried to find humor in things like the size of injection needles or the amount of sperm needed for samples. I remember one occasion when I rushed to make it to a doctor's office before another insemination attempt. As I walked through the door, the doctor seemed surprised to see me. He quipped, "I thought I told you that you didn't have to be here today." I responded, "Doc, if you're gonna get my wife pregnant, at least I'd like to be in the room!"

One pitfall on the trying-to-make-a-baby trail is the sudden realization that everyone around you is getting pregnant. Our college friends, our cousins, other family members, business partners and church friends—they were all having babies. We babysat when people went on vacation, we attended baptisms and arranged baby showers, all the while silently hoping it would someday be our turn.

Heather remembers standing in the checkout line of a supermarket having terrible thoughts about a woman behind her, just because she happened to be pregnant. *How come she can get pregnant and we can't? What's wrong with us?* The questions had no answers. It seemed so unfair. We began to question God and His plan for our life. These were long years.

In retrospect, we see that the trials of infertility were simply part of God's preparation for us as parents. All of the despair, hope, frustration, joy, pain, anger, fear and love was worth something. Now we can appreciate the truth of the Scripture "In all things God works for the good of those who love him" (Rom. 8:28).

APPLYING FOR PARENTHOOD

There are many ways to adopt children. You can go overseas, or you can go to an adoption agency, a social care agency or an attorney. In our neighborhood, we have friends who have been to China twice to adopt children. For them, going to China was an adventure and they loved it. We have another friend who went to Korea to adopt a child. A business associate of mine went to Russia and came back with three children. Another friend found his two children through an agency in Texas. We also have friends who put an ad in a newspaper and found their baby that way. These friends aren't wealthy, nor did they hire some fabulous attorney. None had prior knowledge of foreign countries and their adoption laws. They all just had a passion to be parents, so they started exploring.

In our case, we did a little homework on adoption. (See the Resources section of this book for some good sources of information about adoption.) Then we decided to pursue an open adoption because we wanted phone calls and personal meetings with the birth families.

When we first met Sara, we were right at the end of the infertility treatments. She came to our home and the first thing she said was, "So why haven't you tried in vitro fertilization?" That sort of threw us for a loop. I said to myself, *I thought this lady was coming here to talk about adoption.* Actually, she was. She just wanted to be sure we were ready for what lay ahead, giving us our first little adoption test. Adoption isn't for everyone, and she was probing to see if we were having second thoughts. I'm glad she did that.

As our adoption journey began, we were faced with the challenge of writing the "Profile." As a prospective adoptive parent, you are trying to tell your life story to a person you don't know—in one page. I think we did 50 drafts of that thing. You want to sound serious but not desperate. You want to express your faith (we are Christians), but you don't want to be preachy. You want to say you have a nice home for the child, but you don't want to brag. You want to show that your marriage is great and that you really love each other, but you don't want to be too sappy or transparent.

You also need to include a picture of yourselves that conveys the right message. We decided to use a picture of ourselves that had been taken by a lake where we had recently vacationed. It showed the two of us dressed casually with smiles on our faces. We did not include pictures of our house; the family dog, Molly;

the potential baby's room or the grandparents and cousins. Some people really want to show pictures of those things in the hope of revealing more about who they are. It makes sense. There's no right or wrong way to do your profile. At least in an open adoption, you can say more about yourselves when you meet with the birth family.

It soon became obvious that Sara's idea of open adoption and mine were very different. For me, it meant we would let the birthparents know a little bit about who we were, unlike in the old days when nothing was known of the adopting parents. I felt this was somehow more mature and enlightened. We would exchange pictures, phone calls and maybe a few nice letters a few times a year. Never did I think that Sara would counsel us to meet the birthparents in person.

But before we knew it, Heather and I were on a plane to Chicago, working on our first baby budget and planning what we'd say at a meeting with a couple we'd never met. We met Christine and Jon at a restaurant in a suburban shopping mall, where we talked for about two hours. Christine's parents were there as well as a good friend of hers. In the beginning it was intimidating. We were trying very hard not to say the wrong thing. After all, these people were considering giving us their baby. Before long, the conversation flowed pretty naturally, with the women talking about the pregnancy and we men talking about sports.

Three months later, we were parents! When Dylan was born, we went back to Chicago to bring him home, and it was almost like we were going back to visit family. Everything went well.

We were less intimidated by the process when we adopted our second child, Grace, a short time later. In an adoption agency office near our home, we met with Jennifer (Grace's birthmom) and her mother. Jennifer was still coming to grips with placing Grace for adoption. Appropriately, she wore her emotions on her sleeve. We all made it through, only with lots of hugs and tears. Grace came home with us two months later.

With Brynne, our third child, we were old pros. We met with her birthparents, Joy and Hank, at a local pizza place, and we wore jeans and sneakers. It felt almost like a double date. They were neat young people with whom we had a lot in common. It may sound odd, but we almost felt like a big brother and big sister to those two. Brynne was born about three months after our date with her birthparents.

HOW MUCH OPENNESS?

Open adoption affords an opportunity to better process the emotions for all the parties involved—adoptive parents, birthparents, birth-grandparents, siblings and others.

But even with open adoption, there are differing degrees of openness. All adoptive parents need to consider what level of openness they want before they make an agreement with the birthparents. With our children's birthparents, we enjoy varying degrees of openness.

All of the birthparents get periodic updates from us. It gives us great joy to write the annual letter about the children. We can reflect about the past year's events as well as dream about the future. Because of the letters, we have developed a habit we call "time stamping." Now when we are doing something particularly fun with our kids, we intentionally think of the birthparents. For example, one New Year's Eve we had a nice snowfall, so we built a bonfire in our backyard and invited a bunch of people over for sledding. The children made hot chocolate and s'mores by the campfire. That was an experience we wanted to share in our letters to their birthparents.

You might be thinking, *Don't you ever worry that you might have a problem in the future because of the level of openness you have with the birth families?* Honestly, we do not. Such fear is counterproductive. We feel that we are responsible to love each child unconditionally. If by the time they're 18, they haven't felt loved and they want to go back to their birthparents, then it will only show that we have done a poor job as parents. In my opinion, our openness with the birth families reduces the likelihood of such an event instead of heightening it.

Of course, there is the very real chance that our children will want to meet their birthparents in the future. As daunting as this might sound, it really should be no big deal. If our children want to meet their birthparents, we already have a foundation of trust built with them.

JEALOUS NO MORE

I used to be jealous of couples who could have biological children, but now I think adoption is equally wonderful. Did you ever stop to think about all the things God has to arrange for an adoption? It amazes us how our children found their way to our home.

> *Did you ever stop to think about all the things God has to arrange for an adoption?*

The night we received Brynne, we got a unique glimpse into God's kingdom. At our church, we gathered with our pastor; the birthmother, Joy, her family and some friends; Hank and some of his family. As you might imagine, there was a little bit of friction between these families and some anxiety in the air. Someone had brought a camera and they started taking pictures. It started to feel almost like a wedding. Soon prayer began, and it went on for a long time. Then there were tears, laughter, times of sharing and healing. A situation that had caused so much concern and heartache was being redeemed. As our daughter Brynne was handed into our arms for the first time, everyone in the room was filled with joy. God had orchestrated this adoption.

TO MY CHILDREN

Dylan: The first time we saw you in the hospital, your mother whispered to me, "Perfect in every way." We wrote that on your birth announcements and sent them out to the world. You were our first miracle. Your birth put joy back into our lives.

The tenderness of your heart is what amazes me most about you. God gave you a very special gift of compassion. Never stop trying new things, Dylan. My prayer for you is that you will grow in the assurance that God will never leave you nor forsake you.

Grace: I heard a sermon once that described grace as "a gift that was undeserved." So it is with you, Little Bug. Yours is a silent, contemplative soul. Your quietness belies your true nature. Mom and I say all the time, "That Grace has got game!" Your beautiful, deep brown eyes and glowing smile are your trademarks. Remember, Grace, when you smile, the world does too.

God's gift to you is thoughtfulness. I love watching you take care of your baby sister. You seem intuitively prepared to watch out for her. My prayer for you is that you won't miss the great gift of the saving grace of Jesus Christ. Guess what, Bug, Jesus loves you—even more than I do.

Brynne: Our little catch phrase for you, Baby, is "Someone was missing from the party." A friend of mine thinks we should rename you Grin. That is, of course, because you appear to be the happiest child on Earth. You've joined the clan and you fit right in. Grace and Dylan adore you. We are amazed to see the three of you together.

Your gift from God is happiness. My prayer for you is that you'll never lose that marvelous sense of wonder that you have today. May your heart never be troubled by bitterness, envy or despair and may you rest confidently in the knowledge that God will provide for all of your needs.

Joy's Story

At work one day, I read an article in a magazine about pregnancy. It said that if you were going to the bathroom a lot, sleeping a lot, feeling nauseated, increasing or losing your appetite, or gaining or losing weight, then you might be pregnant. *No!* I thought to myself. *That won't happen to me. That only happens to other people. I just started having sex. Sure, we don't use birth control, but we're careful. Maybe . . . no . . . it just can't be.*

I kept putting it out of my mind until one night when I was at my friend's house. I told Britt that I was scared I was pregnant. She thought it was a false alarm. After all, I hadn't ever had morning sickness and I worked full-time and went to school full-time too, so I must just be tired. But she suggested we go and get a pregnancy test just to put my mind at ease.

We went to the store and got the generic test, the cheapest one available. Back at her house, the test registered negative. But what if it was wrong? I just didn't know what to do. I didn't want to involve my parents! They'd be so ashamed of me. I knew I'd really messed up.

The baby's father wasn't even my boyfriend. Hank was just a friend of mine. If I turned out to be pregnant, I'd have to deal with him, too! I thought maybe I could get an abortion. Or maybe I'd move to Ohio and get a job and have the baby and tell everyone later. Maybe I'd put the baby up for adoption secretly. I just didn't know.

For weeks, I continued convincing myself it wasn't true, even though I did tell Hank I might be pregnant and that he would be the father. The pregnancy test just had to be wrong. But I felt like I was pregnant. I talked to a friend at work and she said she would find out how much an abortion would cost. She said she'd take me to get it done if I wanted. I started crying. *Is this for real? Am I going to abort a baby? Is there a baby? What a mess. How did I let this happen?*

Around that time, I was sitting in church one Sunday when this lady got up to talk. She was from a crisis clinic, talking about unplanned pregnancies. *Great*, I thought. *Does my dad know something?* (He's the pastor of my church.) As she talked, I almost started to cry, but I couldn't make a scene in the front row at church. I took mental notes and then ignored it all for another couple of weeks.

Finally, I had to know for sure if I was pregnant. I went to the crisis clinic to talk to a counselor. She was so sweet. She asked me several questions and gave me a pregnancy test. She confirmed my worse fears. I *was* pregnant. In fact, I was 12 or 13 weeks pregnant. I began to bawl. She asked what I was going to do and I cried again. By this point, an abortion was out of the question, although I don't believe it was ever an option in my heart. I had to choose whether I was going to raise the baby or put it up for adoption. And now I had to start to tell people. I was terrified. This was it. I was going to let the world know about my sin!

I went to a diner with Hank to tell him the news. He was glad I wasn't going to have an abortion. I told my boss. She gave me a hug and let me know that she loved me and supported me in any decision I would make. Then I told my mom. I could hardly get the words past the lump in my throat. My whole body was trembling as I said, "I'm so sorry, Mommy, I'm pregnant." She looked at me lovingly and gave me a hug and said that she and Daddy knew it was bound to happen to one of us four girls. I was really surprised. I didn't think she would handle it that well. She didn't even cry. She told my dad, and he left a rose and a letter on my desk at home. I started to cry the minute I saw it. In the letter, my dad told me that he will always love me. There was much more in the letter about his love but also about his heartache. We had a family meeting later that week to tell my sisters the news.

My parents had a lot of questions, such as, How come you had sex? How many times? Did you have sex in our house? Why couldn't you wait? I didn't want to answer those questions, but I felt I had to. I was the one who had messed up. We talked about adoption and parenting. They said they would support me if I wanted to keep the baby, but they would not raise the baby for me. I understood and agreed. Then they went on to tell me that I was not allowed to hang out with any of those friends anymore. That made me angry. I felt I needed my friends now more than ever. But I was living in my parents' house and that was their new rule.

My dad put in a resignation at the church, although the church didn't accept it. I quit my job as a cheerleading coach at the Christian school my sisters attended. I had to write a letter to my church explaining my situation and asking them not to blame my family for my mistakes. A letter was also sent home to the parents at the school explaining my situation. Talk about a public affair! This was not something that could be dealt with quietly. I received cards from members of the church, and people would come up to me and hug me, people I didn't even know. I just wanted to be left alone. I was overwhelmed. I got depressed. All I seemed to do was go to work and school and deal with being pregnant, go home and sleep and cry.

My parents wanted the family to go to counseling. I agreed that I would do it, but only if I got to pick a counselor that I somewhat liked. That was difficult. Finally, my dad told me about Sara and how she works with pregnant teenaged girls. He thought she'd be someone I could stand. I thought I'd give her a chance. I talked to Hank and he agreed to go to counseling with me. We met with Sara and we thought it would be a good match. We also liked the idea that she could help us find an adoptive couple privately instead of going through an adoption agency.

We started meeting fairly frequently, discussing all of our options. None of this was simple in the least. Hank wanted to raise the baby with me, and I wanted to release the baby for adoption. Every day was a struggle. Not only was I having to deal with a boy who wanted to marry me and raise the baby and live this "wonderful life" that I knew was a fantasy, but I also had to worry about everyone else too. I had to be careful about where I went, everything I ate and drank (for the baby's sake), the father's feelings and my family's feelings—before I could even stop to think of myself. I kept trying not to say anything negative to people because I was trying to be perfect to make up for my previous mistakes. I didn't think I should contradict them. Hank was upset with me for not wanting to raise the baby together, my sisters were upset with me for being pregnant, my mom was upset with me if I didn't do exactly what she thought was best.

The time came for Hank to make his decision, whether he would agree with the adoption or fight me for the chance to parent. When a girl is pregnant she has full rights to the baby—until it is born. After birth, the father and mother have equal rights. This meant that although I was the one who was pregnant, the one who had decided not to abort, and who had decided that adoption was best, it didn't really matter what I wanted if Hank said no. All he had to do was oppose signing the papers and it wouldn't happen. We argued about it.

I didn't think Hank was ready to be a dad. He still lived at home, struggling to hold down his job, and yet he thought he was ready to raise a child. I remember one day in counseling, Sara asked him what he was going to do when he wanted to go out with his friends on weekends but couldn't because of the baby. He said, "I can give up my weekends until the baby is grown!"

Sara responded, "And when's that?"

"You know, two or three years old."

Sara laughed. "Are you kidding me? You're 22 and you still live at home and your mom is still taking care of *you!* This is for life!" He just didn't get it.

Finally, after weeks and months of agonizing worry, stress and anger, he agreed to an adoption. So Sara pulled some references from her files for us to look at. We were finally on our way to picking a family! Then Hank changed his mind again. He vacillated back and forth several more times, but we went ahead and met with a couple of families anyway.

As soon as I met the Gallaghers, I knew that they were the family. It was just a gut feeling. I fell in love with them. Hank really liked them too. We told Sara how we felt and discussed a second meeting with them and their two other adopted children. Sara set it up and we went out with them to lunch. We wanted to see how they interacted with their children. That was it—we wanted the Gallaghers to raise Brynne. (They picked her name because I didn't learn her sex until she was born, and I didn't want her to have a different name after she was adopted.) Sara told the Gallaghers, although everyone knew that Hank was still shaky about his decision.

Finally the day came when I went to the hospital. Hank and Britt came and so did Heather Gallagher. Brynne was born.

After 72 hours, we signed the adoption papers and had a ceremony with the adoptive parents, their pastor, Sara, my family, and Hank and Britt and their families. We prayed, cried and celebrated Brynne's birth and future with her new family. When the time came for Hank and me to actually hand Brynne to the Gallaghers, I had a strange feeling in my stomach. This was it, for life. We handed her over and cried again, but my tears were tears of joy.

My biggest hope for Brynne is that she will grow up knowing that I didn't abandon her. I released her because she deserves a family, not a potential divorce situation with her parents fighting and resenting each other and possibly her. I love her so much, and I know I did the right thing. I love receiving pictures of her. She is so beautiful and full of life.

Chapter 18

We Chose You

Frank F. Lunn

In 1966, I was born as baby "Gary" in an Evanston, Illinois, hospital. After I was adopted, I was renamed Frank Frederick Lunn IV after my adopted father and his father and grandfather. It actually seems strange for me to say "my adopted father," because my adoptive parents have been my real mother and father as far back as I can remember. True, they did not actually conceive me, but there has never been even the slightest hint that I was ever any different from other kids who had "natural" parents.

From day one, my parents were very open and honest about my being adopted. They would always tell me that there were lots of babies and they chose me. They *chose* me! What a proud feeling it is to be chosen and wanted and loved.

I am so very thankful that the woman who is my biological mother cared enough about me to carry me to term and give me the chance to find a loving family. When she found out she was pregnant, I'm sure I was an inconvenience; she may even have thought of aborting me. But ultimately she did the loving thing and treated her pregnancy as a life within her rather than as a situation to be dealt with.

> *I am so very thankful that the woman who is my biological mother cared enough about me to carry me to term and give me the chance to find a loving family.*

Sometimes I wonder how this world would be different had I been aborted as a matter of trivial inconvenience. I think about my mom and dad and my brother and sister and what their lives would have been like without me. I think about my wife and how different her life would be. I guess they could have all survived without me, although their lives would certainly be different. But now I am the father of three wonderful children who wouldn't be alive had my birthmother made a different choice. It makes me thankful beyond words that my mother had the heart to treat her pregnancy like a real life and the courage to carry me throughout her entire pregnancy and then give me up for adoption to a loving family who looked at me as a gift from heaven.

Two years into my life, my parents adopted again and I was blessed with a sister. We grew up with normal sibling issues. We were always a close family with no apparent differences from other families in which the babies came from the "mommy's tummy." My sister and I knew beyond a shadow of doubt that we were loved. Our parents shared openly the fact that they had chosen us and that we were a natural family together. Although neither my sister nor I were born into the family, we were raised as a family.

Apparently, my parents tried to conceive when they were first married, but it just never happened for them. There was no real explanation; it just never happened, so they adopted us. Interestingly, when I was 14 and my sister was 12, our mom got pregnant and we had a baby brother! We continued to have our ups and downs like all families, but we were always one family.

WHAT I WANT OTHERS TO KNOW ABOUT ADOPTION

For parents considering adoption:

> Even though your decision to adopt may be filled with doubts or questions and you will certainly have challenges as all parents do, you can make a wonderful difference in creating a life for a child in need of loving parents. It is not a decision to enter into lightly, but it is one that can certainly change the world for that child.

For young girls who are pregnant right now:

> You may feel like your life is ruined, but I can assure you

it is not. I want you to know that your pregnancy, whether planned or an accident, means you have a human with great potential inside of you. Your life may be a mess right now, but it will get better. Give your baby the gift of life and the chance to grow up with parents who really want your child and will love him or her. You will get your own life back, and you will know that you made a wonderful decision.

I am in my late 30s as I write this. As I look back on my own situation, I would say to my own birthmother, "Thank you for loving me enough to keep me in your care until you gave me up to a loving family." To my own loving family, I say, "Thanks for telling me and showing me with your love, *We chose you!*"

Resources

ABORTION

Forbidden Grief: The Unspoken Pain of Abortion
by Theresa Burke, Ph.D.
Read this book to find out why women can't talk about their abortions and how they can find help and healing for unresolved postabortion grief. It includes personal insights from hundreds of women who have been counseled by the author, who is the founder of Rachel's Vineyard postabortive counseling ministries.

Abortionfacts.com. www.abortionfacts.com
This is an abortion megasite. It includes information from many different sources and looks at abortion from every angle.

Rachel's Vineyard. www.rachelsvineyard.org
Help for the woman suffering from the aftermath of abortion. To help with the healing process, it is filled with helpful links, book recommendations and weekend retreat listings.

Silent No More Awareness. www.silentnomoreawareness.com
For women who have been hurt in any way by abortion.

ADOPTION

Meditations for Adoptive Parents
by Vernell Klassen Miller and Esther Rose Graber
The perfect gift for adoptive parents. Using her family experiences, Vernell Klassen Miller includes theories about bonding to infants

and older children, the stages of relinquishment and adoption, the process of entitlement and the advantages of the adoption process.

The Whole Life Adoption Book: Realistic Advice for Building a Healthy Adoptive Family
by Jayne E. Schooler
This book discusses issues such as what to consider before you adopt, how to tell a child he or she is adopted, how to help your child deal with memories of the past, how to understand the issues and behaviors that can surface in adolescence and how to respond when a child wants to search for his or her biological parents. It offers hope and direction to those considering adoption and those desiring to improve the adoptive family relationships at any stage. For both counselors and counselees.

How to Adopt a Child from Another Country
by Eileen M. Wirth and Joan Worden
This book includes tips for exploring adoption, differences between foreign and domestic adoptions, what to expect realistically regarding cost, creative ways to finance the venture, suggestions for adjusting to the child, a successful case study and listings of foreign agencies by state. For both counselors and counselees.

Adoption.com. www.adoption.com
This one website will link you to many others, all of which are helpful to young women considering adoption as well as parents seeking to adopt.

Adoption.org. www.adoption.org
Adoption.org is a full-service organization that assists both the birthmother and the adoptive couple. Links to other helpful websites.

Bethany Christian Services. www.bethany.org
Represents over 70 Christian adoption agencies and counseling centers. Handles a variety of adoption services, including networking, legal assistance and support materials.

Holt International Children's Services. www.holtintl.org
A Christian international adoption agency. Produces a magazine for adoptive parents.

Liberty Godparent Foundation. www.godparent.org
An organization that maintains a 24-hour crisis pregnancy help line, operates a state-licensed maternity home and a state-licensed adoption agency and provides information on beginning a crisis pregnancy help line.

CRISIS PREGNANCY

Daddy, I'm Pregnant: One Family's Story of
Turning Tragedy into Triumph
by "Dad Named Bill"
Taken from a minister's journal, this book is about a family who weathered a disaster and experienced God's unspeakable grace and healing in the midst of it. Through all the questions and heartache, the author affirms God's unfailing presence. He speaks about choices that can bring healing and comfort, or bitterness and resentment.

Pregnancy Resource Centers. www.pregnancyresource.org.
Formerly called Crisis Pregnancy Centers, this organization provides information and resources to those who are faced with unplanned pregnancy and offers them someone to talk to.

Ruth Graham Ministries. www.ruthgrahamministries.com
Listen to audio or video clips about life issues, including unplanned pregnancy.

PRO-LIFE

Birthright International. www.birthright.org
Here you can find the same type of help you will find on Care Net (see below). This organization has been around since 1968.

Care Net. www.care-net.org
An accessible and effective abortion alternative organization, daughter ministry of the Christian Action Council. Trains individuals, churches and staff of pregnancy-care centers to provide practical care to women in crisis pregnancies. Produces educational materials, sponsors an annual conference, and publishes a national newsletter.

Catholic Charities. 1-800-CARE-002
This is a ministry of the Catholic Church. It provides services to women in unplanned pregnancies.

Heartbeat International. www.heartbeatinternational.org
An interdenominational association of life-affirming pregnancy resource centers, medical clinics, maternity homes and nonprofit adoption agencies.

Hunter's Chosen Child. www.hunterschosenchild.com
A foundation to aid those who are facing the challenges of unplanned pregnancy.

National Association of Christian Child and Family Agencies.
www.naccfa.org
An association that addresses issues of the family and the child
from a Christ-centered perspective.

The Nurturing Network. www.nurturingnetwork.org
This organization is designed to assist a young woman to carry
her child to term. There are many helpful links on this website.

Option Line. www.pregnancycenters.org
This website will help you find someone to answer your questions immediately. There is someone there at all times for you to
talk to at 1-800-395-HELP.

About the Authors

RUTH GRAHAM

Born in 1950, Ruth is the third child of evangelist Billy Graham. Ruth is a published author and national speaker. She received a degree in religion/communications from Mary Baldwin College and for 11 years served as acquisitions editor for Harper Collins San Francisco. For five years she was donor relations coordinator for Samaritan's Purse International and then took the position of major gifts officer at Mary Baldwin College.

Because of her own teenaged daughter's two pregnancies, she has a heart for young women who face the choices of an unplanned pregnancy. She is open about her experience with her daughter and talks honestly about their choices and struggles. She is an effective and experienced communicator. For many years, Ruth has traveled the country sharing her experience as a source of information and encouragement. Ruth is now collaborating with Sara Dormon; they have developed a resource of choices for women with un-planned pregnancies: forpregnancyhelp.com.

Ruth is the mother of three grown children and grandmother of three. She lives in the Shenandoah Valley of Virginia.

Contact toll free: 888-800-4440
E-mail: ruth@forpregnancyhelp.com

SARA R. DORMON, PH.D.

Sara Dormon is a clinical psychologist specializing in issues sur-rounding women and crisis pregnancies. For the past 25 years, she has worked with young women and their families as they faced an unplanned pregnancy and the choices this situation brings. Her own personal journey has given her this passion and desire to help these young women. She and her family have taken many young women into their home, and she has counseled them through the process. Whether they choose adoption or parenting, she helps them plan and prepare for their choice.

She has been a board member and counselor at the Amnion Crisis Pregnancy Center in Bryn Mawr, Pennsylvania, and has done extensive postabortion counseling. She has done television and radio interviews covering the issues of teen pregnancy, abortion and adoption. Until recently, she had a private practice in Lansdowne, Pennsylvania. Sara is an experienced and humorous speaker who brings a refreshing and honest look at some very difficult issues.

Sara is the mother of three sons and the grandmother to three girls. She lives in a suburb of Philadelphia with her husband, Bill.

Contact toll free: 888-800-4440
E-mail: sara@forpregnancyhelp.com